T. R. Miles is Professor of Psychology at University College of North Wales, Bangor. His previous books include *Religion and the Scientific Outlook, Eliminating the Unconscious,* and *On Helping the Dyslexic Child.*

New Studies in the Philosophy of Religion

General Editor: W. D. Hudson, Reader in Moral Philosophy,
University of Exeter

This series of monographs includes studies of all the main problems in the philosophy of religion. It will be of particular interest to those who study this subject in universities or colleges. The philosophical problems connected with religious belief are not, however, a subject of concern only to specialists; they arise in one form or another for all intelligent men when confronted by the appeals or the claims of religion.

The general approach of this series is from the standpoint of contemporary analytical philosophy, and the monographs are written by a distinguished team of philosophers, all of whom now teach, or have recently taught, in British or American universities. Each author has been commissioned to analyse some aspect of religious belief; to set forth clearly and concisely the philosophical problems which arise from it; to take into account the solutions which classical or contemporary philosophers have offered; and to present his own critical assessment of how religious belief now stands in the light of these problems and their proposed solutions.

In the main it is theism with which these monographs deal, because that is the type of religious belief with which readers are most likely to be familiar, but other forms of religion are not ignored. Some of the authors are religious believers and some are not, but it is not their primary aim to write polemically, much less dogmatically, for or against religion. Rather, they set themselves to clarify the nature of religious belief in the light of modern philosophy by bringing into focus the questions about it which a reasonable man as such has to ask. How is talk of God like, and how unlike, other universes of discourse in which men engage, such as science, art or morality? Is this talk of God self-consistent? Does it accord with other rational beliefs which we hold about man or the world which he inhabits? It is questions such as these which this series will help the reader to answer for himself.

New Studies in the Philosophy of Religion

IN THE SAME SERIES

Published

D. Z. Phillips *Death and Immortality*
Richard Swinburne *The Concept of Miracle*
Vernon Pratt *Religion and Secularisation*
W. W. Bartley III *Morality and Religion*
Jonathan Barnes *The Ontological Argument*
Thomas McPherson *The Argument from Design*
T. R. Miles *Religious Experience*
Ninian Smart *The Concept of Worship*

In preparation

D. J. O'Connor *The Cosmological Argument*
Humphrey Palmer *The Concept of Analogy*
I. T. Ramsey *The Problem of Evil*
Kai Nielsen *Scepticism*
David Jenkins *The Authenticity of Faith: Existentialist Theology and the Problem of the Knowledge of God*
W. D. Hudson *Wittgenstein's Influence on the Philosophy of Religion*
Michael Durrant *The Logic of 'God'*

Religious Experience

T. R. MILES
Professor of Psychology, University College
of North Wales, Bangor

Macmillan
St. Martin's Press

First published 1972 by
THE MACMILLAN PRESS LTD
London and Basingstoke
Associated companies in New York Toronto
Dublin Melbourne Johannesburg and Madras

Library of Congress catalog card no. 72–77775

SBN 333 10275 4

Printed in Great Britain by
R & R CLARK LTD
Edinburgh

I shall therefore assume that I have readers who do not wish to see a righteous cause defended in an unrighteous manner.

KANT

Contents

General Editor's Preface   ix

Acknowledgements   x

1 Aims and Method   1

2 Experiences and Mental Events   9

3 Religion and 'Dualism'   15

4 The Claim to Objectivity   27

5 Experiences without Dualism   33

6 The 'Natural–Supernatural' Dichotomy   45

7 Experience and Commitment   53

Notes and References   61

General Editor's Preface

In this monograph Professor Miles presents a distinctive point of view about religious experience with admirable clearness and brevity. He argues that the significance and value of religious experience remain even if the latter is not regarded as evidence of a supernatural, non-material God.

Stated thus, his view might be mistaken for one widely held and commonly stated by humanists who believe that certain forms of ecstasy or certain traits of character which have arisen in connection with religion are valuable and should, if possible, be fostered in the absence of religious belief. But Professor Miles's view is the more unusual one that the *religious* significance and value of such experiences can be recognised even when they are *not* thought to provide evidence of 'another world'.

The argument to this effect leads the author to discuss a number of philosophical questions and to develop further the notion of religion as 'silence qualified by parables' which he presented in his earlier book *Religion and the Scientific Outlook* (1959).

Professor Miles writes lucidly throughout and illustrates his points from the 'highways' of religious experience. His approach to philosophical problems is a contemporary analytical one and his discussion of the meaning of 'experience' in the expression 'religious experience' or of 'existence' in the phrase 'the existence of God', for example, will interest readers versed in philosophy and be found illuminating by those who come new to the subject.

W. D. HUDSON

University of Exeter

Acknowledgements

I am grateful to Dr W. D. Hudson and Professor D. Z. Phillips for their helpful comments and criticisms. The responsibility for mistakes and shortcomings is, of course, my own and not theirs.

T. R. MILES

Bangor
1971

1 Aims and Method

In this study I shall examine some of the possible uses for the expression 'religious experience', and I shall try to indicate both how this expression is helpful and how it is misleading. On the positive side I shall argue that there is every justification for listening seriously to people's accounts of what they have experienced in trying to come to terms with religious issues, and that for the person concerned such experiences can legitimately influence religious commitment; on the negative side I shall argue that it is a mistake to postulate special entities called 'religious experiences' if these are thought of as 'non-material' in character or as providing recondite information about a 'non-material world'. The 'material'–'non-material' dichotomy, in the form in which it is commonly presented, seems to me not merely useless but positively misleading, and I shall try to show that accounts of religious experience are better off without it.

The attack which I shall be making is thus directed not against the ordinary religious believer (unless, perhaps, he inadvertently enters the philosophical arena), but against certain would-be philosophers who in my opinion are distorting religious truth by bad philosophy.

A common catchword of the present age is the word 'materialism'. One meets it in sermons, in after-dinner discussions, in letters to the press, and even to a limited extent in books and articles on philosophy. Now although in many ways I regard the word as a provocative and misleading one, I do not dispute that in some contexts it serves a useful purpose. For example, it makes sense – and in my opinion is often correct – to say that a particular civilisation or country is too materialistic; this is in effect to say that the people in question set too much store by the so-called 'material' things of life, such as food, clothing and money, at the expense of such things as art and literature. If one wants to say that art and literature are 'non-material' or 'belong to a non-material world', this can be harmless provided it is

1

taken as a figure of speech; and it is conceivable that other justifiable uses for the 'material'–'non-material' dichotomy could be found. What I am concerned to attack is the *philosophical* use of the word 'materialism'. In a philosophical context it stands for the assertion that 'nothing exists except matter'. This thesis is widely assumed to be anti-religious; and many people seem to take for granted that if a religious view of the world is to be defended, it is necessary to 'refute materialism' and establish instead (or at least make probable) the counter-thesis that 'non-material' entities exist in addition to 'material' ones.

Now those who argue in this way often suppose that their position can be strengthened by the so-called 'appeal to religious experience'. Their case might perhaps be stated as follows: 'If you deny that religious experiences occur you are culpably ignoring relevant facts; if you try to explain them away as delusions you are being implausible; yet if they occur and are not delusions, this must surely mean that materialism is not the whole truth.' In what follows I shall try to show that this argument is mistaken and that it is possible to take people's accounts of their religious experiences seriously without becoming involved in the controversial issues of 'materialism' versus 'anti-materialism', 'dualism' versus 'anti-dualism', or 'naturalism' versus 'supernaturalism'. If a person has a moving religious experience, it is unnecessary to re-describe the situation by saying that he has received a visitation from the supernatural world.

I have no wish to indulge in controversy with particular individuals. Lest, however, I should be accused of setting up a man of straw, it is perhaps worth while providing an example of the kind of approach which I wish to attack. Sir Alister Hardy, writing in *The Times* about the work of the Religious Experience Research Unit at Oxford, has put forward views very similar to those which I have just quoted. Thus in the first of his two articles he expresses concern over the widespread belief 'that science has dismissed the spiritual side of the universe as an illusion'.[1] His second article carries the heading 'Exploring the World of the Spirit'; and here he explicitly claims that his studies of religious experience involve 'exploration of this non-material world'.[2] If the argument of this study is correct, however, it can be said in advance as a matter of logic that,

2

whatever the findings of the Research Unit, no conclusion can emerge which will justify statements about 'the spiritual side of the universe' in the required sense. Sir Alister seems to me to have made things gratuitously difficult for himself by posing his problem in these traditional terms.

In arguing against views of this kind, I shall not, of course, be defending materialism or denying that the universe has 'a spiritual side'. What I am attacking is the assumption that religious belief requires any reference to the 'material'–'non-material' dichotomy; and, if this is right, the hoped-for 'refutation of materialism' is a philosophical blunder. Religion, in my view, does not need to be buttressed by any such expedients, and, to adapt the words of Kant, I do not wish to see a righteous cause defended in an unrighteous manner.[3]

To guard against misunderstanding, perhaps I should also try to indicate some of the things which this study is not.

In the first place, it is not an anthology of religious writings, comparable, for instance, with Victor Gollancz's anthology, *From Darkness to Light*.[4] I shall mention various accounts of personal religious experiences, but these are intended as examples to illustrate the discussion, not as devotional readings or contributions to literature.

Secondly, I am not attempting any kind of exhaustive catalogue of religious experiences. I do not doubt that different people have all kinds of different experiences, but it is not my task to survey these in any detail. The passages which I discuss are in fact mostly well-known ones – the vision of Isaiah in the temple, quotations from the Psalms, a passage from the fourth gospel, the account of St Paul's experience on the Damascus road, and various more recent writings. For my purposes there was plenty of material in the highways of religious literature, and I have made no attempt to explore the by-ways or to introduce the reader to texts with which he was unfamiliar.

Thirdly, I have for the most part (the experience of St Paul is perhaps an exception) tended to avoid discussion of *unusual* happenings. This is not a book about ecstasy, such as Marghanita Laski has written,[5] nor is it a book about mystics or mysticism. My choice here is a personal one. I am not one of those who believe that the philosophy of religion can be studied with academic detachment. What one selects for discussion, how one

3

defines one's terms (for instance the key term 'religion'), whether one wishes to retain or change existing ways of looking at the world, whether one chooses this example rather than that – all these things reflect a personal viewpoint; and I doubt if complete detachment is possible even on the doubtful assumption that it is desirable. As far as unusual experiences are concerned – visions, ecstasies and the like – I am prepared to listen sympathetically to accounts of them; but I have no inclination to regard them as more important than the experiences of the ordinary person who tries to live a religious life, and I would strongly contest the view that a full religious life is impossible for those who do *not* have ecstatic or mystical experiences. To me there is so much to wonder at in the familiar things of life – for example that people breathe, grow, talk to each other, and love or fear each other – that I find no need to look elsewhere for things of interest. Moreover, in my day-to-day work as a psychologist there is so much of fascination that I have no wish to study such alleged happenings as telepathy, precognition and clairvoyance; and even if the evidence for such things were better than it is, I am doubtful if their existence would have any significance for religion as I understand it.[6] My interest (I am a Quaker) lies in the personal religious experience of individuals and in the way in which particular expressions of religious conviction have 'struck home' to people or failed to do so; and, as far as I am concerned, the fumbling of my neighbour at a Meeting for Worship will almost certainly be of more religious significance than the *recherché* utterance of someone in a trance. This whole issue is admittedly a matter of personal preference, but if the reader is looking for a book on ecstasy or mysticism he should go elsewhere.

Fourthly, this is not an anthropological or sociological study. In other words I shall not attempt to produce evidence as to the kinds of religious experiences which occur in different parts of the world, nor shall I offer any generalisations about the personal or social conditions which give rise to them.

Fifthly, I shall not be discussing what may be called the 'phenomenology' of religious experiences, i.e. what they feel like to the person who has them. Both William James[7] and Marghanita Laski[8] have written in detail on this subject, and I shall make no attempt at any further contribution.

Finally, although most of my professional work is in the

4

psychological field, I am offering this study as a contribution not to psychology but to the philosophy of religion.

The remainder of the present chapter will be concerned with problems of method. In Chapter 2 I shall critically examine the view which equates experiences with 'mental events'. In Chapter 3 I shall begin by considering some of the different strands of meaning in the word 'religious', after which I shall try to show what I believe to be wrong with traditional discussions about 'dualism' and 'materialism'. In Chapter 4 I shall argue that the so-called 'appeal to religious experience', if regarded as an argument against 'materialism', is misconceived. In Chapter 5 I shall indicate possible uses for the expression 'religious experience' independently of the issue of dualism, while in Chapter 6 I shall indicate some of the mistakes and confusions which occur if one asks whether religious experiences are 'supernaturally caused'. Finally, in Chapter 7, I shall consider the relationship between religious experience and religious commitment. My central thesis is that it is possible to take seriously the notion of personal experience in religion without being involved in discussions about 'materialism', 'dualism' or 'supernaturalism'.

To end this chapter, here is a brief discussion of problems of method. Some readers, particularly those with a scientific training, may wonder how it is that philosophical reflection (or 'armchair speculation', as they might wish to call it) can ever lead to fresh truth. No one disputes that presentation of *evidence* can achieve this; but how, it may be asked, can one hope to say anything new simply by 'sitting and thinking'? Can the inquiry, even at best, be anything more than an elaborate exercise in word-spinning?

There is, I think, one contribution at least which is philosophical in character, viz. to examine the validity of arguments. For example, if it transpires on logical grounds that the inference from 'People sometimes have religious experiences' to 'There exists a non-material world' is unjustified, it is surely a legitimate piece of philosophising to point this out.

I should like to suggest, however, that there is more to philosophy than this; and the following further consideration seems to me of special importance. Many arguments, in particular

5

arguments about religious issues, are often difficult to evaluate because they turn on different ways of interpreting ordinary language.

This point requires elucidation. I am not saying simply that people should be circumspect in what they say and explain the meaning of their terms carefully. This may often be true, but it does not constitute a revolutionary new philosophical technique. Recent philosophers – and I am thinking here of Wittgenstein, Ryle, Austin and their followers – have encouraged us to look at 'ordinary language' for more subtle reasons. Here is a well-known quotation from Austin:

> Our ordinary words are much subtler in their uses and mark many more distinctions than philosophers have realised. . . . It is essential . . . to abandon the deeply ingrained worship of tidy-looking dichotomies.[9]

The suggestion here is that, if we look really carefully at language, this forces us to study how one situation (where we say such-and-such, say A) is like or unlike another situation (where we use a different expression, say B), and how both are partly like a third situation where we are not sure whether the expression A or the expression B is more appropriate. Careful examination of 'what we would say if . . .' can make us sensitive to important similarities and differences and hence can sharpen our awareness of what is the case.

Perhaps a problem of biological classification will serve as a reasonably simple example. In the course of biological work the question may arise as to whether the duck-billed platypus is a mammal or a bird. To answer this question we need both to know what are the facts, i.e. know all the respects in which it is like and unlike typical mammals and typical birds, and also to reflect on the logical (or 'conceptual') point of what is entailed by the sentences 'X is a mammal' and 'X is a bird' in the ordinary use of these words. Applying Austin's expression, 'the deeply ingrained worship of tidy-looking dichotomies', one might say in this case that ordinary experience justifies the 'tidy-looking dichotomy' of 'mammals' and 'birds', but that the words which we use do not always do full justice to the complexity of every situation; thus the facts about the duck-billed platypus are such that it cannot be classified without reservation either as a mammal or as a bird. In this particular example –

6

and indeed in many others – the important thing is not so much one's final decision on what to say as the working-out of all relevant similarities and differences.

In brief, ordinary language *classifies*. Hence one can say that an important task of the philosopher is to decide whether or not to recommend revision of existing classifications. As Austin has emphasised, however, a caveat is necessary here: before proposing any revision we need to be completely clear what it is that we are revising. As will be seen more fully in Chapter 4, if this precaution is not observed, there is danger that we may be hoodwinked by misleading analogies, false contrasts and concealed shifts in the meaning of the words which we are using; and one way in which the philosopher can influence classificatory decisions is to point out that such errors have taken place.

A particularly striking exposure of such mistakes is to be found in Ryle's book, *The Concept of Mind*.[10] For instance, he argues in chap. 1 that in many philosophical contexts the contrast between an entity called '*the* mind' and an entity called '*the* body' is a false one, while in chap. 5 he brilliantly exhibits the effect of a misleading analogy:

> People often pose such questions as 'How does my mind get my hand to make the required movements?' and even 'What makes my hand do what my mind tells it to do?' Questions of these patterns are properly asked of certain chain-processes. The question 'What makes the bullet fly out of the barrel?' is properly answered by 'The expansion of gases in the cartridge'; the question 'What makes the cartridge explode?' is answered by reference to the percussion of the detonator; and the question 'How does my squeezing the trigger make the pin strike the detonator?' is answered by describing the mechanism of springs, levers and catches between the trigger and the pin. So when it is asked 'How does my mind get my finger to squeeze the trigger?' the form of the question presupposes that a further chain-process is involved, embodying still earlier tensions, releases and discharges, though this time 'mental' ones.[11]

Finally, he speaks in the same chapter of philosophers' 'unwitting extension of the ordinary sense of "voluntary"';[12] here the suggestion is that unnoticed shifts in meaning lead to

7

misclassifications and failure to distinguish things which are different.

One of Wittgenstein's examples is that of the philosopher who unwittingly tampers with the meaning of the expression 'cannot really be sure'. Such a philosopher might argue: 'Pain is something private to each individual; we can never therefore really be sure if someone else is in pain.' These words, however, as Wittgenstein in effect points out, incorrectly imply a similarity with those situations where a person keeps a stiff upper lip and conceals his pain. 'Just try', he says, '– in a real case – to doubt someone else's fear or pain.'[13] In another passage he says: 'When philosophers use a word – "knowledge", "being", "object", "I", "philosopher", "name" – . . . one must always ask oneself: is the word ever actually used in this way in the language-game which is its original home? What *we* do is to bring words back from their metaphysical to their everyday usage.'[14]

Here is no place to follow up in detail the problems raised by philosophical discussions of this kind. The main point, I think, is that if we fail to take seriously what is implied by the words of ordinary language we may unwittingly misclassify and hence mislead ourselves. The philosopher's contribution, it seems to me, is not just to evaluate arguments but to evaluate classifications; and a necessary starting-point is thus to look at the classifications implicit in ordinary language.

The justification for this technique will, I hope, become apparent in later chapters. One of my main tasks will in fact be to take up Wittgenstein's challenge by calling attention to the everyday uses of the word 'experience'; and I shall try to show that its sophisticated uses involve a misleading shift of meaning. If I am right, it becomes necessary to reconsider some of the things which we might otherwise have said about specifically *religious* experience. In particular I shall argue that we should not think of religious experiences as 'mental' entities as opposed to 'physical' ones, nor as devices for putting us in touch with a 'non-physical' or 'non-material' world. To talk in this way is to misclassify.

2 Experiences and Mental Events

In this chapter I shall not be concerned with specifically religious experience, but I shall make some comments on the notion of 'experience' in general. I shall suggest that sophisticated people have tampered with the ordinary uses of this word and have thereby distorted the facts, thus generating unnecessary disputation.

An important source of the trouble, so I shall claim, has been the equation of 'experiences' with 'mental events'. There is an amusing passage in *The Concept of Mind* in which Ryle ridicules the person who makes this mistake. Such a person, he says, 'is likely . . . to speak glibly of "experiences", a plural noun commonly used to denote the postulated non-physical episodes which constitute the shadow-drama on the ghostly boards of the mental stage'.[1] In what follows I shall begin by calling attention to some of the absurd consequences which arise if the word 'experience' is construed in this way. I shall then go on to exhibit some of the ways in which it functions in ordinary usage. This is not, of course, because I regard ordinary usage as sacrosanct but because we are likely to mislead ourselves if we change ordinary usage unwittingly.

As an illustration of the sophisticated use of the word 'experience', here is a passage from an introductory psychology textbook by E. G. Boring and colleagues:

> It can be made obvious to everyone that personal experience can be observed immediately. If we hold a pencil up before the mirror the immediate experience is that of two pencils. Here we have a datum of mind or consciousness. . . . When the direct observation of phenomenal experience is being employed in psychological experimentation . . . the occurrence of the term *observer* . . . gives notice that the introspective method is in use. . . . There have been many theories of the relation of phenomena to events in the brain. . . . John B. Watson . . . tried to oust phenomena from psychology.[2]

9

Three claims seem implicit in this passage: first (a) that experiences are in some sense 'data of mind or consciousness'; secondly (b) that it makes sense to speak of 'directly observing' experiences; and thirdly (c) that it makes sense to argue whether 'phenomenal experience' should or should not be included in the subject-matter of psychology. Although the climate of philosophical and psychological opinion has appreciably changed since the original publication of this passage (1936), the mistakes which it embodies still seem to me to be sufficiently interesting to merit discussion.

(a) The first suggestion is that experiences are 'data of mind or consciousness'. Those who speak in this sophisticated way of 'mind or consciousness' imply that these two concepts are basically similar. If, however, we consider ordinary usage before sophisticated thinkers have mauled it about, a more complicated picture emerges. In ordinary speech 'conscious' is sometimes contrasted with 'unconscious', sometimes with 'inanimate'. A person may be knocked unconscious; an anaesthetist may wonder if his patient has recovered consciousness; and one may say of oneself 'I was conscious of faint noises in the distance', 'conscious of' here being equivalent to 'aware of'. Where the word 'inanimate' is used, on the other hand, as it is, for instance, of sticks and stones, this implies that the contrast between 'conscious' and 'unconscious' is not applicable. Passing now to the word 'mind', we find that its uses are many and varied. Thus there are expressions such as 'He has an astute mind' and 'He is absent-minded'; and there are many different uses for the dichotomy between 'physical' and 'mental'.[3] An important characteristic possessed by some varieties of living organism – and by man in particular – is the ability to take account of what is not actually present. We may see things 'in our mind's eye', we may do mental arithmetic, and we may be with someone 'in spirit' though not present physically. There is a connection between 'mental' and 'conscious' in that organisms which are capable of being conscious are also capable of taking account of what is not actually present; but to speak of 'mind' and 'consciousness' without consideration of the many different ways in which these words function in ordinary speech is to blind ourselves to important distinctions; and, as Ryle has in effect pointed out,[4] to suppose that the whole universe consists of either mental existents or physical existents is to blind ourselves still further. In this connection Austin's warning against 'the worship of tidy-looking dichotomies' (p. 6 above) seems particularly pertinent.

Had the attention of Boring and his colleagues been called to these points, I do not think they would any longer have wanted to say that an experience is 'a datum of mind or consciousness'.

(b) They also speak of 'the direct observation of phenomenal experience'. In saying this, however, they do not seem to me to have thought out what part is being played by the word 'phenomenal'. The contrast is presumably not between 'phenomenal' experience and some other kind of experience; but in that case it is not clear that the word 'phenomenal' in this context adds anything at all. It does, of course, make perfectly good sense to speak of 'describing one's experience', and there is even a use for the somewhat sophisticated words 'phenomenology' and 'phenomenological'; thus one might say that a phenomenological account of an experience is a description of how things looked, sounded or felt at the time when the person was having the experience. There is also an intelligible contrast between 'phenomenal' and 'physical'; thus one might wish to contrast what the subjects in a psychological experiment say in describing their experiences (e.g. 'a bright moving circle') with what the experimenter says in describing the stimulus in physical terms, i.e. in the units of physics such as lamberts, centimetres or seconds. To speak, however, of 'phenomenal experience' seems at best redundant, since any description of experience is presumably a description of 'phenomenal experience', and at worst confusing, since it says by implication that there could be non-phenomenal experiences.

According to Boring and his colleagues phenomenal experience is sometimes 'directly observed'. This seems to me to be a very curious thing to say. Clearly there is a use for 'I have just observed a butterfly'; but I cannot easily think of a use for 'I have just observed an experience'. Moreover, it makes sense to ask 'Did you observe the butterfly directly?', if the implied contrast is that of observing through a mirror or periscope;[5] but even if it made sense at all to speak of observing experiences, it is particularly hard to see what kind of sense could be attached to the notion of observing them either directly or indirectly.

(c) They treat as a live issue whether one should 'oust

11

phenomena from psychology'. This is the traditional issue of whether or not psychologists should be behaviourists. It seems clear from the context that the following words and their derivatives are being treated as belonging in the same family: 'mind' (with the derivative 'mental'), 'phenomena' (with the derivative 'phenomenal'), 'conscious' (with the derivative 'consciousness'), and 'experience'. Hence the issue is posed in terms of whether we should consider mind as well as body, the mental or phenomenal as well as the physical, and consciousness and experience as well as behaviour. This notion of a great divide, with 'mind', 'conscious', 'phenomenal' and 'experience' on the one side, and 'body', 'physical' and 'behaviour' on the other, represents a grotesque oversimplification of how these terms function; those who think in this way are blinding themselves to important differences and condoning a shift of meaning in the word 'experience' which they have failed to recognise.

As a result of this shift, sophisticated thinkers have been led to make a contrast between 'experience' on the one hand and 'behaviour' on the other, 'behaviour' being characterised as the 'physical' movements of an organism and 'experience' being something 'mental'. On the assumption that 'experience' and 'behaviour' are contrasting terms, psychologists have then gone on to argue whether psychology should study experience *and* behaviour or behaviour only. More careful attention to the word 'experience' would cause this problem to disappear.[6]

There is a further complication if 'experiences' are equated with 'events of consciousness' or 'mental events': one must necessarily be assailed by sceptical doubts as to how we can ever be aware of a world outside or beyond the events of our consciousness. Further experiences can serve to check mistakes in perception – illusions, hallucinations, etc.; and it is quite legitimate from one set of experiences to infer that others will follow. It is a very odd kind of inference, however, which leads, not from one set of experiences to another, but from experiences to something which could not in principle ever be experienced! The whole starting-point seems to me to lead inevitably to solipsism, i.e. the view that nothing exists except oneself, since experiences on this showing are *one's own* experiences and from the nature of the case there can be no legitimate inferences to anything further. This sceptical conclusion arises from the misconstruing of the word 'experience'.

12

I conclude, therefore, that those who have equated 'experiences' with 'mental events' have introduced an innovation without being aware that they were doing so, and that the result is gratuitous confusion.

Our next task is to examine the non-philosophical uses of the word 'experience', or, as Wittgenstein would say, look at its uses in 'the language-game which is its original home' (cf. above, p. 8).

If we consider the expressions '*An* experience of . . .', '*The* experience of . . .' and (simply) 'Experience of . . .' (or '*Any* experience of . . .'), we find that the missing blank can be filled in a variety of ways. A person may have an experience of peace or inward joy; he may have the experience of being loved or hated; he may have had experience of hardship, hunger or pain; and he may have had experience of teaching or mountaineering. There is also the expression 'experience *with* . . .' (as opposed to 'of'); thus one might ask if someone had had experience with children or with soldering-irons; similarly people can have or lack political experience. These examples show the variety of uses to which the word 'experience' can be put. There is perhaps an analogy with the word 'happen': happenings, like experiences, are of many different kinds, and it is not clear that they necessarily have some one feature in common.

The non-specific nature of the word 'experience' can also be illustrated by the fact that one does not 'have' experiences *simpliciter*, in the way in which one 'has' twinges of indigestion or toothache. 'Have you had any experiences recently?' is a strange question in a way in which 'Have you had any twinges of indigestion recently?' is not. The strangeness disappears, however, if something specific is added, e.g. 'Have you had any *exciting* experiences recently?'

We need also to consider if there are any situations where the expression 'experience of . . .' is followed by a proper name. If the proper name occurs on its own, without addition or qualification, I can think of none. One can ask someone if he has ever had an experience of happiness or disgust, but it would be odd to ask him in the same tone of voice if he had ever had an experience of Smith. What one experiences is something *about* Smith; thus it makes sense to say 'My experience of Smith

13

is that he talks non-stop' or 'I have had a lot of experience of Smith' (i.e. I am used to the kinds of thing Smith does); but in reply to the question 'What did you experience last night?' it would be odd to say 'I experienced Smith'. This is a point to which we shall return when we consider the phrase 'an experience of God'.

It is also worth calling attention to the kinds of adjective which usually precede the word 'experience'. Thus experiences can be described as 'remarkable', 'exciting' or 'new', but not as 'pink', 'square' or 'fluffy'. In this respect the logical behaviour of the word 'experience' is different from that of words descriptive of familiar objects such as 'table' or 'house', since adjectives of colour, shape and texture are clearly applicable in the case of tables and houses. If we say that words such as 'pink', 'square' and 'fluffy' refer to qualities, it is plain that 'remarkable', 'exciting' and 'new' do not refer to qualities in the same way; or perhaps it would be more correct to say that they do not refer to single qualities and not necessarily to the same qualities on all occasions. What a new pair of shoes has in common with a new tennis racquet is not anything to do with, for example, brightness (though many new things do in fact shine); what the two have in common is that both are being used for the first time or thereabouts. Similarly there is no one single quality of 'remarkableness' nor a single quality of 'excitingness'; things can be remarkable or exciting for many different reasons. Sometimes the adjective before the word 'experience' delimits the area or subject-matter that the person was concerned with, as when we speak of 'a musical experience'. This situation is, of course, quite unlike that in which one describes, say, a child as musical. A musical child is one who has musical ability, whereas experiences do not have (or lack) musical ability; a musical experience is what one experiences in listening to music.

The main purpose of this chapter has been to contrast the sophisticated uses of the word 'experience' with the unsophisticated ones. My conclusion is that if we equate 'experiences' with 'mental events', as sophisticated philosophers and psychologists have done, we shall generate confusion. I shall suggest in what follows that, for an adequate understanding of the expression 'religious experience', it is the unsophisticated uses of the word 'experience' which need to be taken into account.

14

3 Religion and 'Dualism'

For the sake of clarity I shall begin by commenting on some of the different strands of meaning in the word 'religious'. To make such comments is not a distinctively philosophical activity, since I am not concerned, as I was in the case of the word 'experience', to exhibit any philosophical misclassification; but in many kinds of inquiry discussion of what one means by a word is often a desirable preliminary.

In the case of the word 'religious' the issue is complicated by the existence of what may be called 'evaluative overtones'. For example, there is a passage in Lucretius[1] where he argues that scientific knowledge can liberate, whereas religion prompts people to wickedness. He quotes as an illustration the story of Agamemnon's sacrifice of Iphigenia which was carried out to gain the favour of Artemis, and he concludes his account with the well-known words:

> Tantum religio potuit suadere malorum.
> ('Such evil deeds could religion prompt.')

There is a passage in similar vein in Holbach, the French eighteenth-century philosopher and scientist:

> Nature invites man to love himself, incessantly to augment the sum of his happiness: Religion orders him to love only a formidable God who is worthy of hatred; to detest and despise himself, and to sacrifice to his terrible idol the sweetest and most lawful pleasures. Nature bids man consult his reason, and take it for his guide: Religion teaches him that this reason is corrupted, that it is a faithless, truthless guide, implanted by a treacherous God to mislead his creatures. Nature tells man to seek light, to search for the truth: Religion enjoins upon him to examine nothing, to remain in ignorance. Nature says to man: 'Cherish glory, labour to win esteem, be active, courageous, industrious': Religion says to him: 'Be humble,

15

abject, pusillanimous, live in retreat, busy thyself in prayer, meditation, devout rites, be useless to thyself, and do nothing for others.' Nature tells children to honour, to love, to hearken to their parents, to be the stay and support of their old age: Religion bids them prefer the oracle of their God, and to trample father and mother under their foot, when divine interests are concerned. Nature commands the perverse man to blush for his vices, for his shameless desires, his crimes: Religion says to the most corrupt: 'Fear to kindle the wrath of a God whom thou knowest not; but if against his laws thou hast committed crime, remember that he is easy to appease and of great mercy: go to his temple, humble thyself at the feet of his ministers, expiate thy misdeeds by sacrifice, offerings, prayers.' Nature says to man: 'Thou art free, and no power on earth can lawfully strip thee of thy rights': Religion cries to him that he is a slave condemned by God to groan under the rod of God's representatives.[2]

Now one's first reaction to these two passages may be to say that both Lucretius and Holbach were hostile to religion, and that defenders of religion would take a different view. Closer scrutiny, however, may suggest instead that the matter is not so much one of disagreement as one of verbal misunderstanding. Thus a religious believer might say on reflection, 'This is not genuine religion but a caricature', and by way of rejoinder he might quote the following passage from the Epistle of James:

The kind of religion which is without stain or fault in the sight of God our Father is this: to go to the help of orphans and widows in their distress and keep oneself untarnished by the world.[3]

Others, however, might point out that there is nothing particularly *religious* about helping widows and orphans, since a humanist (in the sense of someone professing opposition to religion) would equally regard it as his duty to offer such help.

Clearly there is some kind of dispute here as to how the word 'religion' should be used. What is less clear is whether this dispute is important.

To throw light on the matter, I should like to call attention to the term 'persuasive definition', which was introduced into philosophy by C. L. Stevenson.[4] This is in effect a definition

16

which combines explaining the meaning of a word with an expression of the speaker's own values. One of Stevenson's examples is the case of someone, B, who says to another person, A: 'In the true and full sense of the term, "culture" means imaginative sensitivity and originality.' Stevenson continues: 'It will be obvious that B, in defining "culture", was not simply introducing a convenient abbreviation, nor was he seeking to clarify "the" common meaning of the term. His purpose was to redirect A's attitudes.'[5] A well-known example of a persuasive definition of religion is offered in Fielding's *Tom Jones*: 'When I mention religion,' says Mr Thwackum, 'I mean the Christian religion; and not only the Christian religion, but the Protestant religion; and not only the Protestant religion, but the Church of England'.[6]

Now there is no objection in principle to persuasive definitions as such; indeed without them an important means of expressing our values would be closed to us. In this particular case one may object to Mr Thwackum's values on the grounds that he is bigoted and narrow-minded; but this is an objection not to persuasive definitions but to the particular views which Mr Thwackum is commending. The important point logically is that we should not mistake persuasive definitions for arguments, since as arguments they would be question-begging. This can be illustrated by examples from other fields. Thus if someone says, 'We ought always to inflict something unpleasant on lawbreakers because otherwise *it wouldn't be punishment*', this assertion masquerades as an argument when in fact the central question (whether we should always punish in the sense of inflicting something unpleasant) is begged. Again, if someone says, 'What the present Government is offering isn't real conservatism', this is a logically unobjectionable expression of a view; but if it were offered as an argument – 'the Government ought not to be doing what they are doing *because* this is not conservatism' – the speaker could rightly be accused of begging the question. Similarly sentences of the form, 'True religion is . . .', are not *ipso facto* objectionable, but they become logically vicious if the speaker then tries to justify his position by adding 'because that is what the word "religion" means'.

Now persuasive definitions sometimes imply persuasion in favour, sometimes persuasion against. Thus for the majority of English-speaking people at the present time I think it likely that

17

the word 'democratic' has persuasion-in-favour overtones' whereas the word 'authoritarian' has persuasion-against overtones. (There is in fact a technique devised by C. E. Osgood and his colleagues[7] for the systematic study of how people react to the overtones or 'connotative meaning' of a word; but details need not concern us here.) What is unusual about the word 'religion' is that some people use it intending persuasion-in-favour overtones and others use it intending persuasion-against overtones; and this does not make for ease of communication. There is an additional complication in that not all practising Christians are on the persuasion-in-favour side and not all professed anti-Christians on the persuasion-against side. Christians on the persuasion-against side are likely to speak in favour of 'religionless Christianity' and to say that Jesus Christ came to *rid* the world of religion, while anti-Christians on the persuasion-in-favour side are likely to plead in favour of a 'religion of humanity'. It is logically unobjectionable for a believer to 'give away' the word 'religion' to his opponents, and it is a trivial matter – indeed, as some would say, a 'purely verbal' matter – whether one opts in the first place for a persuasion-in-favour or a persuasion-against sense of the word 'religion'. Once one has opted, however, it matters a great deal how the word 'religion' is then defined, since one is thereby expressing a view as to what is good or bad. It follows that we need to look at the context to determine whether a particular dispute about the meaning of the word 'religion' is 'purely verbal' or not.

As far as this study is concerned, there are three strands of meaning in the word 'religion' which I wish to distinguish. In the first place a religious person may be thought of as one who believes in God or in some more-than-human power; secondly, he may be thought of as one who performs certain rituals, including in particular acts of worship; thirdly, he may be thought of as one who holds certain 'cosmic' views, i.e. views about the nature and destiny of man.[8] In most versions of Christianity all three of these ideas are present together. The important one, however, in my opinion, is the last one. Belief in a God is one answer to these cosmic questions, and performance of appropriate ritual may be important as a consequence. It is the cosmic questions themselves, however, which seem to me to present the crucial challenge at the present time. My use of the words 'religion' and 'religious' is thus persuasive (and,

18

in fact, persuasive-in-favour), since I am defining the word so as to emphasise a particular feature of its accepted usage which seems to me important.

Here are some examples of what I have in mind in speaking of 'cosmic' questions. 'What is man', asks the psalmist, 'that thou are mindful of him?';[9] 'Whence are we and what are we?', writes Shelley in *Adonais*:

> . . . of what scene
> The actors or spectators?

FitzGerald's version of *The Rubá'iyát of Omar Khayyám* contains many discussions of such issues:

> Into this Universe, and why not knowing,
> Nor whence, like Water willy-nilly flowing:
> And out of it, as Wind along the Waste,
> I know not whither, willy-nilly blowing.

I have no wish to lay down any general rules as to how the word 'religion' should or should not be used; but as far as this study is concerned I shall be discussing people's experiences in trying to come to terms with cosmic questions.

One final source of misunderstanding requires mention. I still continue to meet those who believe that modern philosophy has put these cosmic or ultimate questions 'out of court' by declaring them to be 'pseudo-questions'. I do not dispute that the notion of a 'pseudo-question' may sometimes be helpful. Indeed it seems to me, for example, that the question 'How can I ever tell if someone else is in pain?' (when asked in a philosophical context) can correctly be called a 'pseudo-question' for reasons given on p. 8 above. Again, if someone interested in perception asks, 'Why does the world not look upside-down since the image on the retina is inverted?', I think it can be shown that this, too, is a pseudo-question, though the reasons are too complex to be discussed here. Cosmic questions, however, seem to me quite different; in particular the recognition that in some cases they have logical peculiarities does not make one any less inclined to ask them. To take a particular example, I do not dispute that the question 'Who am I?', when asked in a cosmic sense, is logically strange. This can be shown by calling attention to possible non-cosmic uses: for instance, a person who had lost his memory might ask 'Who am I?', needing to

19

be reminded of his name and way of life; in this case he is not asking anything of cosmic significance. It seems to me, however, that it is possible to be aware of this kind of example and yet still to want to use the words 'Who am I?' in a cosmic sense, even though they are perhaps more like a cry of bewilderment than a straightforward question.

Our next task is to take up the points raised in Chapter 2, and examine how far they can elucidate the notion of specifically *religious* experience.

If experiences in general are equated with 'mental events', it follows that religious experiences are a special kind of 'mental event'. This seems, for instance, to be the view of E. S. Waterhouse, who asserts that 'religious experience consists of psychical states'.[10] It also seems implied in the view of F. E. England when he says that the investigation of religious experience 'is primarily concerned with subjective events and processes'.[11] If the argument of Chapter 2 is correct, however, it is misleading, and indeed mistaken, to suppose that the word 'experience' can function in this way. Neither religious experiences nor other kinds of experience should be thought of as events in a 'non-material' world.

This kind of mistake is the more tempting because of the many distinctive things which are true of human personality. People can fall in love; they can enjoy art and music; they can recognise compelling demands; they can ask and attempt to answer cosmic questions. If to do these kinds of thing is to have a 'spiritual' nature, then I am certainly not denying that man's nature is 'spiritual'. Indeed, it seems to me plain that human beings are in important ways different from animals and that both, again, are different in important ways from computers. (The human brain is, of course, in certain ways *like* a computer; but if a computer were devised to do everything which the human brain could do, I would not conclude that the human brain was 'a worthless thing' but that the computer was a particularly exciting one.) I am not disputing that cosmic questions are different from scientific ones, or that questions of what we ought to do in particular situations are often very complex; indeed, if phrases such as 'a spiritual world', 'spiritual values', etc., are used in a context where appropriate distinctions are being drawn, then they present no problem.

20

What I am attacking is in effect a gratuitous complication introduced by philosophers. The ordinary religious believer has no need to talk about the distinction between 'material' reality and 'non-material' reality. Among philosophers, however, this distinction has acquired the status of a 'grand dichotomy', as a result of which everything has to be classified either as 'material' or as 'non-material'. I should like to suggest instead that there are all kinds of classifications for all kinds of different purposes. The respect which we owe to human beings is in no way conditional upon the existence of this 'grand dichotomy'.

What is misleading is the postulation by philosophers of a 'spiritual world' (in a context where 'spiritual' is equated with 'non-material') and the further assumption that 'religious experiences' are either entities belonging in this world or devices for putting us in touch with such a world. At the risk of seeming to caricature my opponents, perhaps I should expand on this point. According to the view which I am attacking, the 'spiritual world' is thought of as a shadowy counterpart to the ordinary familiar world of people and things; and just as a person via the 'material' side of his nature – his eyes, ears, central nervous system, etc. – can pick up signals as to what is happening in the 'material' world, so, it might seem, a sensitive person who is 'spiritually' attentive can pick up signals from the 'non-material' or 'spiritual' world. On this showing, of course, those who assert that only the material world exists are displaying unjustified arrogance and dogmatism.

It is, I think, no accident that many of those who talk in this way are also interested in the possibility of so-called 'extra-sensory perception'. Their hope seems to be to establish, either from card-guessing experiments or from well-attested 'spontaneous' happenings, that 'mental events' are not merely different from 'physical events' but do not even require a physical basis. For example, it might be thought positive evidence of 'extra-sensory' powers if one person, A, correctly indicated what cards another person, B, was looking at when no ordinary perceptual cues were available to him, such as a direct sight of B's cards or some means of inferring them. Even if the factual evidence for such occurrences were sufficient, however, there still seems to me to be a very dubious logical link between 'A scored "better-than-chance" in a card-guessing experiment' and 'A is perceiving certain events in the absence

21

of any physical basis'; and any further inference to the effect that A must therefore be a 'spiritual' being or belong to a 'spiritual world' seems to me entirely unwarranted. In this area the 'conceptual' issues, i.e. issues of *what we are entitled to say*, are, I think, quite as problematic as the factual ones. In technical psychological journals experimenters do not ever – to my knowledge – report that they have controlled for the possibility of extra-sensory perception; thus it would seem that in practice, whatever they profess, they do not take the possibility of extra-sensory perception seriously. My personal belief is that they are right not to do so. Even if they are wrong, however, I cannot see how such positive evidence would establish more than that some people have surprising powers of telling what is going on; and to use this alleged fact as some kind of buttress for religious belief seems to me logically unjustified.

The basic assumption behind all the views which I am criticising is that, if one is to take religion seriously, one is necessarily committed to a 'dualist' view of the world, a view, that is, which states that the world contains two kinds of entity, material entities and non-material ones.

In what follows I shall challenge this dualistic account, not by coming down on the side of materialism, but by exhibiting the mistakes which arise if one formulates one's problem in these terms at all. Religious belief, in my opinion, requires no such 'non-material' story. What is called for is not the assertion that these 'non-material' entities exist nor the equally unarguable counter-assertion that they do not exist, but careful reflection on the way in which words are being used. Those who have carried out such reflection will, I am sure, hesitate before posing their problems in this traditional way.

If my argument is correct, it follows that the very phrase 'religious experience' may have misleading associations. I would even say that in so far as it implies this mistaken view it requires to be abandoned. 'Those experiences which put us in touch with non-material reality' is as unsatisfactory a form of words as 'Those experiences which put us in touch with square circles'; in both cases alike we are misleading ourselves and have failed to reflect adequately on what our words mean. Such an interpretation carries the further implication that the experiences in question must be unusual and (quite literally) out of this world; and it is therefore small wonder that certain down-to-

22

earth persons assert that they 'don't have' religious experiences.

Once the mystifying verbiage is cleared, however, the notion of 'religious experience' becomes perfectly intelligible. A person can describe his *religious* experiences – that is, his experiences when he tries to come to terms with cosmic issues – in the same way logically as he can describe, for instance, the experiences which he had last summer in Norway; in neither case does it make sense to ask if his experiences were mental events or if they made him aware of something non-material. People's experiences of trying to live a religious life can of course be very varied, and examples of such experiences will be given in Chapter 5.[12]

The first stage in my argument will be to elucidate the term 'dualism'. This can best be done, I think, by means of an example; and for illustrative purposes I shall consider what was said by the French philosopher and mathematician, René Descartes. The following is one of the relevant passages:

> I thence concluded that I was a substance whose whole essence or nature consists only in thinking, and which, that it may exist, has need of no place, nor is dependent on any material thing; so that 'I', that is to say, the mind by which I am what I am, is wholly distinct from the body, and is even more easily known than the latter.[13]

One of the key words in the above passage is 'substance'. To understand this notion we need to go back to Aristotle, and to consider in particular his doctrine of the *categories*.[14] What he says may be summarised as follows: if we take the words 'Socrates is . . .' and then leave a space, there are various types of word which can appropriately follow. For example, one can say *what* Socrates is, viz. a man: this is to apply the category of substance; one can say that he is of such-and-such a height: this is to apply the category of quantity; one can say that he is wise: this is to apply the category of quality, and so on. Aristotle lists ten different 'categories' in this sense; and if we call what is said of Socrates a 'predicate', then categories, for Aristotle, are different *types of predicate*.

Now it has been widely held that the category of *substance* is distinctive in a special way. The Greek for 'substance' is in fact *ousia*, and this word is connected with the root *onto-*, meaning

23

'existence' or 'being', from which the word 'ontological' is derived. The suggestion seems to be that we are entitled to use expressions such as 'really exist', 'actually exist', 'is real' etc., only in connection with words belonging in the category of substance. Thus the words 'man', 'house' and 'stone', one might say, stand for things which 'really exist' in a way in which the words 'wisdom' and 'tallness' do not. We do, of course, use the verb 'to be' with abstract nouns such as 'wisdom' and 'tallness' (e.g. 'There was much wisdom in the ancient world'); but it does not follow that wisdom and tallness are special *kinds of existent* comparable with men or houses or stones. To use a philosophical technical term, their 'ontological status' is different.[15]

The justification for calling Descartes a dualist, then, is that he believed that there were two different kinds of substance, thinking substance (*res cogitans*) and extended substance (*res extensa*), and that these were of different 'ontological status'.

Now it is no part of my programme to argue that all questions about 'ontological status' are misguided, but I shall try to show that in some contexts they can be.

Here are some trivial examples of ontological differences. The words 'Wednesday', 'justice' and 'off-side' are none of them substance words; one might ask, for example, whether there was a cottage on a certain island but not whether there was a Wednesday or an off-side next to it. Again, in providing someone with a drink I might use a cup and reach out towards him, but it would be odd to say that I used both a cup and a reach, since this would imply that the words were of the same ontological status. Similarly, I might use margarine for cooking and a crawl-stroke for swimming, but the words 'margarine' and 'crawl-stroke' are ontologically different.[16]

Next, here are some examples which are of philosophical importance. On the basis of the argument in Chapter 2 of this study, it can, I think, be claimed that the word 'experience' is ontologically *dissimilar* from the word 'behaviour'; and, if this is right, it follows that arguments as to whether psychologists should or should not study experience *in addition to* behaviour are misguided (cf. above, p. 12). Again, it is always likely to be of interest to discuss the ontological status of new scientific concepts as they arise – 'magnetic field' or 'the unconscious', for example. Here one needs to look with special care at the situations where these words are used. Thus to discover the unconcious is in important ways unlike discovering a new continent (though some psychoanalytic writings perhaps blur the difference), and a magnetic field is in important ways unlike a field which grows crops. Another example of an interesting ontological question is that of placing the word 'God'. Much popular thinking assumes that one can ask whether there exists a God *in addition to* ordinary familiar objects. Much depends here on the way in which one wishes to use the word 'God'; but if we take seriously what has been said about God by theologians, for example, that he is a being 'than which greater cannot be thought',[17] it follows that to discuss whether God exists or does not exist in a straightforward sense (as one might discuss whether dodos or sea-urchins exist) is a philosophical blunder. This is a point to which we shall return (pp. 49 *seq.* below). All I am trying to say at present is that ascription of words to the correct ontological category can be of extreme importance.

Some philosophers, however, seem to me to have made a fundamental mistake over these ontological questions. They have asked, 'What kinds of entity are there in the universe?' in much the same way as one might ask for a list of furniture in a room. They have asked whether material objects exist, whether minds exist, whether numbers exist, and whether God exists, as though they were asking for an inventory of 'things which exist'. This is what I have referred to in an earlier work as 'the *absolute-existence* mistake.'[18] As Warnock has aptly put the matter, 'The question . . . is frankly assimilated to such questions as whether there are lions at Whipsnade or trams in Edinburgh'.[19] Once again consideration of unsophisticated usage may help us. If my wife asks me what I want for supper I might well reply, 'What is there?' This clearly means, 'What is there for supper?' I should in that case be very surprised if my wife then said, 'Don't you realise – you've just asked the central ontological question!'[20] It is this alleged 'central ontological question' which seems to me to be a non-question. One can ask, 'What is there?' or 'Does so-and-so exist?' *in a particular context*, e.g. 'What is there for supper?', 'Does there exist a prime number between 25 and 30?', 'Do there exist any duties which are absolutely overriding?'; but to ask questions about 'existence' when no context at all has been given is to mislead ourselves

25

with words, and it is this which constitutes the 'absolute-existence' mistake. I shall show later (pp. 30–2 below) the absurdities which follow when this mistake occurs in discussions of religious experience.

There is an amusing passage in Kant where he castigates those who offer a bad answer to a meaningless question, 'thus presenting, as the ancients said, the ludicrous spectacle of one man milking a he-goat and the other holding a sieve underneath'.[21] Some of the current discussions of dualism seem to me to suffer from precisely this defect. I am not saying that, throughout the history of philosophy, no uses can be found for the word 'dualism'. It is clearly of interest, for example, that the language of physics, which includes references to electrons, fields of force, etc., is in many ways different from the language of common sense in which we speak of the familiar things of our experience – chairs, birds, sunsets, and flowers; and if someone chooses to say that there are therefore 'two kinds of reality', with suitable caution this could be harmless. What I do say, however, is that in much present-day discussion 'dualism' is cited as a possible answer to the question, 'How many kinds of entity are there in the universe?', and that, if this is the question, it is a misguided one. If I am right, then *any* answer to it is inappropriate; one is equally incorrect to assert that only 'material' realities exist and to assert that 'non-material' or 'spiritual' realities exist in addition.

It is scarcely surprising that those who attempt to argue these matters never make any progress; as a matter of logic it is difficult to see how they ever could. Religion, as I see the matter, does not need to be tied to a 'dualist' world-picture; it is quite possible to take people's religious experiences seriously without raising the issue of 'dualism' at all.

4 The Claim to Objectivity

If, as I have argued in the previous chapter, it is a mistake to ask whether there exists a 'non-material' or 'spiritual' world to addition to 'the material world', then it is also a mistake to suppose that religious experience puts people in touch with such a world.

In this chapter I shall try to press the argument home by exhibiting some of the absurdities which arise if one thinks of religious experience in these terms. I do so by means of a fable.

Once upon a time there were three men, called Euethes (or Simpleton), Invictus and Humanist. They lived on the lower floor of a two-storey block of flats, and none of them could tell for certain who, if anyone, lived in the flat above.

Euethes thought that there was a very powerful *Man* up there. Invictus regarded this idea as very naïve; certainly, on his view, it was not an ordinary 'material' being, and he was in no way discomforted when he learned from the cleaner, Mrs Astronaut, that she had recently visited the flat and found no one there. He still wanted to emphasise, however, that chairs, tables and the familiar trappings of flats were not the only reality; and, while he did not claim to be sure, he declared himself willing to regulate his conduct on the assumption that there was a *non-material* Being in the flat above. This meant that it was important not to make too much noise. Humanist agreed with him on the noise question, though in his case he simply thought noise undesirable; he did not believe there was anyone in the flat above, and the question of pleasing or displeasing such a person did not therefore arise. Despite their differences in outlook, therefore, Humanist and Invictus were happy to co-operate in forming a noise-abatement society. Another point, too, on which they were agreed was in despising one of the recent visitors to the flat, a Mr Facing-Both-Ways, who had declared that 'There is a Being in the flat above' was simply another way of saying 'Do not make too much noise'; according to both of them such a view savoured of sophistry and self-deception.

One day Euethes declared that he had heard some tapping on the ceiling. Humanist was inclined to be sceptical. It was known that Euethes had suffered from epileptic fits and it seemed likely that his claims were the result of his own over-active imagination. Invictus declared himself unsure in this particular case, but he thought it at least possible that the non-material Being might see fit to use tapping as a means of communication with those living below. During the next few weeks a number of their friends visited the flat, and many of them confirmed that they could hear the tapping. Although more than one of the visitors also suffered from epilepsy, there were several who did not, and Humanist's position of plain scepticism became decidedly uncomfortable. In addition he acquired the reputation of seeming arrogant and dogmatic. One of his arguments was that, if there was anyone there, we would surely expect him to reveal himself more often and more convincingly; but Invictus pointed out in reply that one had no right to expect this of anyone, let alone anyone of such obvious standing as a *non-material* Being.

The dispute was never resolved. Invictus would not agree that further visits from Mrs Astronaut, the cleaner, would be relevant; he did not expect her verdict to be anything but negative. But he still thought that these occasional tappings might be evidence of 'something more' or 'something beyond', and he insisted that Humanist was being arrogant and dogmatic in refusing to allow for this possibility. Neither side has convinced the other, and nothing is now left for them except assertion and counter-assertion. There seems no way out of the deadlock.

I have told this somewhat mischievous fable in order to exhibit the sort of way in which the so-called 'argument from religious experience' is often presented. On this showing we are all like the occupants of the lower flat, and the question posed is whether our religious experiences constitute evidence, however fleeting, for the objective existence of a 'non-material' or 'super-sensible' reality.

This issue has often been supposed to constitute one of the

main points of contention between those who call themselves 'Christians' and those who call themselves 'humanists'. For many people in both camps the alleged 'super-sensible reality' is equated with God, and the issue is seen as the straightforward one of whether such a reality exists. If, as I shall argue, it is mistaken to pose the problem in this way, then at least one ground for distinguishing between 'Christians' and 'humanists' disappears.

My argument is not, of course, that the evidence is insufficient. Indeed at no stage has this study been concerned with assessment of evidence. My point is rather that, *whatever* the evidence, it cannot as a matter of logic give grounds for any such conclusion. It makes no sense, on my view, either to say that the evidence is sufficient or to say that it is insufficient; and indeed it is similarly mistaken to declare oneself unsure whether the evidence is sufficient or not.

Invictus, in my fable, accused his opponents of arrogance and dogmatism. Unlike Humanist, however, I do not wish to make any counter-claim, whether arrogant or otherwise. An Invictus-type account of religious experience is wrong, on my view, not because it involves a mistake in the facts or their interpretation but because if we accept it we are deceiving ourselves with words. There is nothing arrogant in reflecting on the meaning of words and then refusing to pose the problem in a particular way; and if one can show, as I hope to do, that a particular view involves misleading analogies, false contrasts and concealed shifts of meaning, then the reasons for rejecting it are logically compelling. Such rejection is no more arrogant than refusal to believe in married bachelors.

I shall argue that in this particular case the analogy of 'whether there is someone in the flat above' is misleading, that the contrast between 'material' and 'non-material' serves no useful purpose, and that those who say that the source of religious experiences must be some 'objective reality' have unwittingly shifted the meaning of the word 'objective' and have in fact failed to give it any meaning at all.

'Does the tapping have an objective source?' asks Invictus. According to the view which I am attacking, precisely the same kind of question can be asked about religious experiences. In some cases, perhaps, they are subjective and illusory, and to be accounted for by saying that the person is mentally disturbed, while in other cases they are genuine. The two situations, however, are not as similar as they appear to be. There is a perfectly good use for the 'subjective'–'objective' dichotomy (or for the 'illusory'–'verdical' dichotomy) in the case of the fable of the top flat, since criteria are available for distinguishing the two. A buzzing in my head is different from a buzzing caused by a bee; the buzzing of the bee is 'objective' in the sense that both I and others can be aware by independent criteria, viz. sight and touch, of the presence of the bee, whereas if the buzzing is 'subjective' these criteria will not be satisfied, nor will a buzzing in my head be picked up by a tape-recorder. But Invictus has insisted that his view is *not* that of Euethes; he certainly does *not* wish to say that we can verify that God is the source of the religious experience by seeing or touching him or investigating whether his voice can be picked up on a tape-recorder. If he wishes to discuss the issue using the 'subjective'–'objective' dichotomy, the onus is on him to give a meaning to these terms, since it is plain that 'objective' cannot bear its ordinary sense, confirmation by seeing, touching or using a tape-recorder having been ruled out.

There is, of course, no law against using words in a new sense; but if one does so unwittingly one is misleading oneself. In this particular case one is presupposing a similarity with the man-in-the-top-flat situation when no such similarity exists.

Invictus may reply by saying that this objection is a disguised form of materialism. 'You are assuming', he might say, 'that the only things which exist are those which can be seen and touched or can act physically on recording devices. Why should not a "spiritual" or non-material Being be the source of these experiences? You have no right to say that such a Being does not exist.'

To say this, however, is only to shift the mistake from the word 'objective' to the word 'exist'; it is Invictus who is couching the problem in these terms, and it is up to him to explain himself. A brief answer to his objection is simply to say that in talking in this way he is making the 'absolute-existence' mistake (see above, p. 25). At this point, however, it may be helpful to look more fully at what is involved. In particular I should like to call attention once again to the different categories of word with which 'exist' is regularly enjoined. Thus, to quote the examples already given on p. 25, it makes sense to ask if there exists a prime number between 25 and 30 or if there exist any duties which are absolutely overriding. I see no logical impropriety in either of these questions; and if Invictus' charge is that I am, for instance, denying that there exists a prime number between 25 and 30, this is plainly false. If this is not his charge, however, he has failed to make clear what he means. I am making no claims about what does or does not exist; it is he who has introduced the dichotomy between 'material' and 'non-material', and my challenge is simply to ask him what distinction he is trying to draw in using this pair of terms. If he – or any of us – is to claim that a non-material Being exists, we must be prepared to say what *difference* the existence of such a Being would make, or, perhaps better, what is achieved by the language which asserts his existence. One might at first be tempted to answer that such language tells us what we shall discover with our senses; but since this possibility has already been ruled out as inapplicable, it is hard to see what remains. Talk of such a Being does not tell us something mathematical, as does 'There exists a prime number between 25 and 30', nor anything about what we ought to do, like 'There exist some duties which are absolutely overriding'. If the suggestion is that the existence of such a Being is postulated in the way in which a physicist might postulate the existence of a magnetic field, then those who say this should make clear what can be achieved by such language which cannot equally well be achieved without it. To say 'I believe that there is *something*, but not something observable, and not something whose existence makes or could make any difference at all to anybody in any way' is surely to emit empty verbiage; and those who protest against such talk cannot be accused of making arrogant claims about what does or does not exist, since they are simply trying to avoid muddle and self-deception.

Finally, even if it made sense to talk of an 'objective source' of religious experiences, there would still be a difficulty in identifying this source with 'God'. In this connection we need to bear in mind once again the theological claim that God is a being 'than which greater cannot be thought';[1] and it is hard to see how a Being postulated as 'the objective source of religious experiences' could satisfy this requirement. At most one would have inferred some kind of origin for religious experiences and given it a name. The man in the top flat in our fable was one being among others, whereas by definition this cannot be true of a Being 'than which greater cannot be thought'. Those who argue that there must be a god in order to account for our religious experiences are failing to take seriously the view that God is not just one existent among others.

I conclude, therefore, that the analogy with the man-in-the-top-flat situation breaks down as soon as we start to examine it closely.

5 Experiences without Dualism

My purpose so far has been to try to show that we should not think of religious experience as a special means of gaining access to a 'non-material' reality. The next task is to consider what can be said on the positive side. For this purpose it will be helpful, I think, to reconsider the ordinary uses of the word 'experience' rather than the sophisticated philosophical ones.

As we saw on p. 13, people can have experience of all sorts of things – of teaching or mountaineering, with children or with soldering-irons; they can have or lack political experience; they can enjoy exciting musical experiences or undergo moving experiences in the solitude of a mountain.

To describe one's experiences as a teacher is to describe what it is like to be a teacher. The situation with regard to religion seems to me to be logically similar; a person, for example, who became converted to Christianity might describe his experiences both before and after conversion, and in particular his experiences in trying to come to terms with cosmic questions.

Are we to say, then, that these are *religious* experiences? In some ways, as we have seen, the expression 'religious experience' is unsatisfactory. It is uncomfortably tied in with the 'material'–'non-material' dichotomy, and may be thought to carry the implication of unusual or out-of-this-world experiences. If these associations are discounted, however, there is nothing against its use in the present context. Further clarification is needed, however, of what such use involves.

We have already noted (p. 14 above) that it makes no sense to speak of experiences as being, for example, pink, square or fluffy. Now in some contexts the word 'religious' has logical affinities with adjectives such as these which describe qualities. For example, the expressions 'a tall man' and 'a religious man'

33

have something logically in common; just as tallness is a spatial quality, one might say, so religiousness is a quality of character, both terms alike being applicable to people. An experience is not religious, however, in the same sense in which a person is religious; one is not saying that the experience has certain qualities of character, any more than one would say that it had the quality of tallness. We can speak of a common quality (tallness, fluffiness, etc.) which *objects* share, but it is a mistake to look for a quality or combination of qualities shared by experiences in general or by religious experiences in particular. Precisely this point was in fact made many years ago by William James, when he said: 'There is religious fear, religious love, religious awe, religious joy, and so forth. . . . There is no ground for assuming a simple abstract "religious emotion" . . . present in every religious experience without exception.'[1]

Another possibility is to consider whether one can assimilate the expression 'religious experience' to the expression 'musical experience'. In both cases, certainly, we are indicating the subject-matter of the experience or the general area with which the experience is concerned – in the one case religion, in the other case music. Moreover, just as a passage of music may suddenly take on a new and exciting significance, so some particular religious writing or ritual or perhaps some ordinary everyday event may take on a special religious significance. Religious experiences, on this showing, are logically similar to musical experiences.

In one important respect, however, the similarity does not hold. There are experts in music – those who by experience and training are entitled to speak with authority. In contrast, sensitivity on religious issues calls for no similar expertise. One may listen to a fresh pronouncement by a religious teacher the more seriously because one respects some of his earlier pronouncements, but in the religious sphere there are no doctorates or academic fellowships for 'experts' and no agreed criteria by which such distinctions could be awarded. It is therefore incorrect to appeal to the 'expertise' of the religiously sensitive in the way in which one legitimately appeals to the expertise of a qualified musician.

So far we have considered the notion of 'religious experience' only in a very general way. It may perhaps be helpful at this stage to consider particular examples. These are not comprehensive; and indeed one needs, I think, continually to bear in mind William James's title, *The Varieties of Religious Experience*, since it emphasises that religious experiences can differ from one another in all kinds of ways. If they are to count as 'religious', however, then at the very least they will share in common a concern with cosmic issues.

This point needs further clarification. One might feel a certain obligation – to visit a sick person, perhaps, or to support a particular cause – without this being a matter of *cosmic* concern; similarly one might be very much moved by a broadcast talk, a piece of music, or the kindness of a friend, without considering it to have any *cosmic* significance. On the other hand any such happening – or indeed any happening – might take on such significance to a particular person on a particular occasion. Where this happens, the situation becomes 'charged with the grandeur of God';[2] and where demands are made, these take on a special kind of seriousness and present themselves with an insistence – a nagging insistence, one might say – which carries its own compelling character.

There is one further preliminary point. Answers to cosmic questions do not occur *in vacuo*; they arise in the context of a particular religious tradition with its own particular practices, symbols and world-picture.[3] As examples, therefore, I shall quote accounts of experiences which have occurred within the framework of Western Christianity and the pre-Christian Judaism from which it arose.

I begin with one of the most telling descriptions of a religious experience which I have ever met:

> In the year of King Uzziah's death I saw the Lord seated on a throne, high and exalted, and the skirt of his robe filled the temple. About him were attendant seraphim, and each had six wings; one pair covered his face and one pair his feet, and one pair was spread in flight. They were calling ceaselessly to one another,
>
> > Holy, holy, holy is the Lord of Hosts;
> > the whole earth is full of his glory.
>
> And, as each one called, the threshold shook to its foundation, while the house was filled with smoke. Then I cried,

35

Woe is me! I am lost,
for I am a man of unclean lips
and I dwell among a people of unclean lips;
yet with these eyes I have seen the King,
    the Lord of Hosts.

Then one of the seraphim flew to me carrying in his hand a glowing coal which he had taken from the altar with a pair of tongs. He touched my mouth with it and said,

See, this has touched your lips;
Your iniquity is removed,
and your sin is wiped away.

Then I heard the Lord saying, Whom shall I send? Who will go for me? And I answered, Here am I; send me.[4]

Now we should never lose sight of the fact that this experience of Isaiah's took place in a setting where the Hebrew view of the world was taken for granted. The young Isaiah claims to have seen Jehovah. It is true that the last sentence quoted, 'Here am I; send me', could be transferred as it stands into a present-day context with the minimum of strain. Indeed it seems to me likely that anyone with a sense of vocation, whatever his religious background and the age in which he lived, would find these words significant. The fact remains, however, that this experience occurred in a Hebrew context; and to accept the importance of 'Here am I; send me', while allowing the references to Jehovah and the seraphim to fall into the background, seems to me to distort the significance of the whole passage. It is as though one tried to summarise the teaching of Jesus by citing the parable of the Good Samaritan while ignoring what he said about the law of Moses, the kingdom of God, the behaviour of devils, and indeed all those things which made sense to his contemporaries but which seem alien to us in the twentieth century. That the story of Isaiah in the temple requires to be 'demythologised' if it is to have a message for us today – this I do not dispute; and the same holds in the case of the New Testament narrative. Nothing is gained, however, by pretending that the mythology is not there; and in the case of any religious experience it seems to me important that one should try to understand the historical setting in which it occurred.

Here is no place to discuss in detail the notion of demythologising; but it may be helpful if I offer a few words by way of explanation. The term owes its origin to the biblical scholar, Rudolf Bultmann,[5] and the following account seems to me to summarise the essentials of his view:

The New Testament, he says, presents redemption in Christ as a supranatural event – as the incarnation from 'the other side' of a celestial Being who enters this earthly scene through a miraculous birth, performs signs and wonders as an indication of his heavenly origin, and after an equally miraculous resurrection returns by ascent to the celestial sphere whence he came. In truth, Bultmann maintains, all this language is not, properly speaking, describing a supranatural transaction of any kind but is an attempt to express the real depth, dimension and significance of the *historical* event of Jesus Christ. In this person and event there was something of ultimate, unconditional significance for human life – and that, translated into the mythological view of the world, comes out as 'God' (a Being up there) 'sending' (to 'this' world) his only-begotten 'Son'. The transcendental significance of the historical event is 'objectivised' as a supranatural transaction.

The above summary is the work of John Robinson,[6] who has himself taken over what seem to be some of the more important of Bultmann's ideas and used them for his own purposes. Here are two passages from his more popular writings which seem to me to illustrate clearly how Robinson wishes the term 'demythologising' to be understood, and they indicate the sense in which I am using the word in this study:

Many today are put off by a way of thinking which was no stumbling-block at all to the men of the Bible. They naturally thought of God as 'up there' or 'out there', and the idea of a heavenly Being 'sending' his Son to this world was perfectly acceptable to an age which thought of gods paying visits to the earth. This is where you looked for reality to be revealed. But to most people today that just seems fanciful, and makes the whole Christmas story sound like a fairy-tale. I am much more concerned that it shall sound like the reality it is than that we should preserve the time-honoured pictures. . . .

Then there are all the 'tinselly' bits of the Christmas story – the star, the angels and the celestial choir. These were recognised ways for the men of the Bible of saying 'God is in all this'. As poetry, I believe, they still have a magic power to take us out of our mean selves. They speak of the mystery of Christmas. But if all they succeed in doing for you is banishing Christ to an unreal world of fairy-lights, then cut them out.[7]

And again:

... What I *am* concerned about is that we shall see the poetry, the myth, for what it is intended to be – a way of describing the meaning, the ultimate, divine significance, of the history – and not as a literal account of *how* things happened. .... I believe that we may have to do a rescue operation on Christmas not simply from commercialism – which ironically gives it one of its few points of contact with the modern world – but from the very artistry that is meant to show its truth. We may, for the time being, have to strip it down, to demythologise, not because we don't believe but precisely so that we can.[8]

With these points in mind, let us pass to a well-known passage in Micah:

What shall I bring when I approach the Lord?
How shall I stoop before the God on high?
Am I to approach him with whole-offerings
    or yearling calves?
Will the Lord accept thousands of rams or ten thousand
    rivers of oil?
Shall I offer my eldest son for my own wrongdoing,
my children for my own sin?
God has told you what is good;
and what is it that the Lord asks of you?
Only to act justly, to love loyalty,
To walk wisely before your God.[9]

Here, too, the requirement 'to act justly, to love loyalty' is timeless and can be applied at the present time without strain; but the demand to people to 'walk wisely before [their] God' clearly belongs to a particular religious tradition.

An important notion in Christianity has often been that of

38

personal religious experience. Thus it seems plain that the writer of the fourth gospel is continually inviting his readers to consider what Christ means to them in their own personal lives. The comments attributed to the Samaritans are particularly relevant in this connection: 'They told the woman, It is no longer because of what you said that we believe, for we have heard him ourselves.'[10] This particular challenge was taken up by George Fox in the seventeenth century. Institutionalised religion, on his view, was likely to be barren unless its tenets had been verified in the experience of the believer. Thus he is reported as having said to his audience, 'You will say, Christ saith this, and the apostles say this; but what canst thou say?'[11] It is no accident that the opening section of the Quaker book, *Christian Faith and Practice in the Experience of the Society of Friends*, is entitled 'Spiritual Experiences of Friends'; and the emphasis on personal religious experience has remained a fundamental part of the Quaker tradition right up to the present time.

Here is an account of Christian experience from a quite different source:

> The humbler phenomena of which we are here thinking are the direct and normal manifestations of sincere religious feeling: conversion to the faith and moral conversion; the special firmness of the adhesion to faith . . .; fidelity to a very elevated moral ideal, the interior touches of that 'grace' of every moment, which makes the Good more luminous and sustains effort; . . . serenity . . . under trials; the specifically Christian humility of mind and heart – in short, the daily religious life, imperfect with some, better organised and fuller with others.[12]

The author, Father Maréchal, is in fact writing about mysticism, but he emphasises, correctly in my opinion, that meaningful religious experiences are not just the prerogative of those who are thought of as mystics.

My last two examples both seem to me to count as 'religious experiences' although the imagery used is not that of traditional Christian orthodoxy. The first example is taken from Francis Thompson's poem, *The Hound of Heaven*:

> I fled Him down the nights and down the days;
> I fled Him, down the arches of the years;

I fled Him, down the labyrinthine ways
Of my own mind; and in the mist of tears
I hid from Him, and under running laughter.
  Up vistaed hopes, I sped;
  And shot, precipitated,
Adown Titanic glooms of chasmed fears,
From those strong feet that followed, followed after.

My second example is taken from Emily Brontë's *Last Lines*:

O God within my breast,
Almighty, ever present deity,
Life that in me has rest
As I, undying life, have power in thee.

Vain are the thousand creeds
That move men's hearts, unutterably vain,
Worthless as withered reeds
Or idlest froth amid the boundless main,

To waken doubt in one
Holding so fast by thine infinity,
So surely anchored on
Thy steadfast rock of immortality . . .

Just as a person may give an account of his experiences as a teacher or of his experiences when travelling the world, so these writers have given us an account of what they experienced on the religious side. No further elaboration is needed from me; this language speaks for itself.

I do not see any good reason for further delimiting the meaning of the term 'religious' or the term 'cosmic'. If this were done, it would be possible for all experiences to be unambiguously labelled 'religious' or otherwise; but very few terms other than the technical ones of mathematics and science have this kind of precision. Indeed in any problem of classification nothing is gained by assigning marginal cases to one category rather than another unless one has looked in detail at all relevant similarities and differences; and the question 'Does such-and-such an experience genuinely count as religious or not?' may well serve as a reminder that in a particular case we need to scrutinise these similarities and differences very carefully. There are often advantages in keeping language flexible rather than imposing systems of classification on ourselves in advance.

What is plain is that none of the experiences cited involve the language of dualism. Indeed whether there are or are not two kinds of substance, material substance and non-material substance, seems at best a matter of abstract speculation, far removed from anyone's personal religious experience; and if my argument is right, it is not even intelligible speculation but empty verbiage. No one will find the 'material'–'non-material' distinction in Isaiah or indeed elsewhere in the Old Testament; in the New Testament we learn that God is *pneuma* ('spirit')[13] just as we learn that he is light[14] and love,[15] but the idea of a 'non-material Being' is foreign to all biblical thought. I do not dispute that accounts of religious experiences can sometimes be found (particularly in post-eighteenth-century writings) which presuppose dualistic ways of thinking, but to assume that for a believer in Christianity dualism is *necessary* seems to me quite mistaken; and in the passages quoted above from Maréchal, Emily Brontë and Francis Thompson dualistic language is noticeably absent.

It was suggested earlier (p. 13 above) that there does not appear to be any obvious use for the expression 'I had an experience of Smith last night', though it makes sense to speak of 'an experience of Smith's talkativeness'. This is in contrast with, for example, the expressions 'an experience of happiness' or 'an experience of disgust', where nothing is needed by way of amplification. The question therefore arises as to what sense, if any, can be made of the expression 'an experience of God'.

C. B. Martin[16] considers the case of a believer who says 'I had a direct experience of God' on a particular date. The difficulty which I feel about this statement is that it does not seem to me to be the statement of a believer at all, but rather that of a sophisticated philosopher speaking without reference to any actual situation. It is intelligible to me that someone should feel himself in the presence of something holy; it is even intelligible, in the light of our knowledge of Hebrew thought, that Isaiah should describe his experience in the temple as a direct encounter with Jehovah. What is not intelligible is a sentence which is manifestly similar to 'I had a direct experience of Smith' except for the substitution of 'God' for 'Smith'. It is perhaps open to

Martin to argue that the word 'God' is logically different from the word 'Smith' and is not in this context functioning as a proper name. In that case, however, the sentence 'I had a direct experience of God' simply does not mean what it purports to mean; and there is no evidence in this passage that Martin is aware of any such shift in meaning. It is hard to resist the conclusion that he has misled himself, as indeed have other philosophers, by citing a sentence for philosophical examination without giving it a proper context and without attending in sufficient detail to the things which people actually say.

By way of contrast, it may be interesting to consider a similar form of words which has actually been used by someone in a religious setting. I am referring to Vaughan's famous line:

> I saw eternity the other night.

Certainly 'I saw eternity' can justifiably be considered an odd expression; 'eternity' is not a word which one would normally expect to find as the object of the verb 'see'. There is no law, however, against oddities of this kind, and no one is misled by Vaughan's line, whereas it is self-deception to philosophise about seemingly religious language which no one in fact would ever use.

If we qualify the expression 'experience of God', then these difficulties disappear, just as they did in the case of the expression 'experience of Smith' (p. 14 above). 'Thy loving kindness and mercy shall follow me all the days of my life' says the psalmist.[17] In this context one might well speak of experiencing God's love or his mercy, and logically this is exactly comparable with experiencing Smith's talkativeness. The thought-forms are of course those of the Hebrew and Christian traditions, and, though one may wish to demythologise, the word 'God' in such a context is still functioning just like any other proper name. It is, of course, not in any way surprising that those who describe their religious experiences should use the imagery of those religious traditions with which they are most familiar.

There is a further use of the expression 'experiencing God' which requires mention. People sometimes say that they can experience God in the slums as well as in the countryside, or in a nuclear explosion as well as in a place of outstanding beauty. In this context, however, 'to experience God' seems to be an elliptical way of saying 'to experience the presence of God'. The

42

claim is thus that even in the most unlikely situations a committed person will still be disposed to say, 'Truly the Lord is in this place, and I did not know it'.[18] There is no reference here to the 'material'–'non-material' dichotomy and no suggestion that in a literal sense a 'non-material' person was present. What is required to make sense of this kind of situation is not literal belief in the presence of a 'non-material' person but willingness to demythologise an account of the felt presence of an ordinary person.

Precisely the same principle applies when people claim to have experienced the presence of some other named individual – the risen Christ, perhaps, or even the Virgin Mary. The naïve account of the situation might be somewhat as follows: 'If the Virgin Mary did in fact appear on such-and-such a date, then X's claim to have encountered her is justified; if she did not, then he was deluding himself.' It seems to me, however, that this form of words is self-defeating. This can be shown as follows: if the sentence 'X recently encountered the Virgin Mary' is ever to be literally true, some kind of identity is necessarily presupposed between the original Virgin Mary who lived almost two thousand years ago and the person whom X has recently encountered. Now in the ordinary way personal identity is guaranteed by the fact of bodily continuity. If we ask whether so-and-so is really the person who disappeared five years ago under the name Smith, part of what is meant is that there has been bodily continuity between so-and-so and the original Smith. Where the criterion of bodily continuity is excluded, however – as must be the case in claims to have met someone who lived in a previous age – it is hard to know what the claim to have met such a person could mean. In particular, if someone asks, 'What is it about the situation which entitles you to say that it was specifically the Virgin Mary whom you met?', no satisfactory answer seems possible. In my more naïve moments I have been tempted to wonder if one could say that some 'non-material' version of the Virgin Mary had survived, but at best this seems to be saying that the usual criteria of identity are not applicable, and unless other criteria are given this does not help. The philosophical problem of personal identity is too big an issue to discuss in any detail here;[19] but the above considerations seem to me sufficient to show that claims to have encountered any person of a previous age, such as the Virgin Mary, are unintelligible if they are interpreted in this naïve way. There is, of course, no self-contradiction in supposing that someone might appear in all respects similar to the original Virgin Mary when she was a certain age and with all the appropriate memories and character-traits, but it would still not be true-by-definition that she was the Virgin Mary; it would be a matter of obtaining a ruling as to whether *enough* criteria of identity were satisfied to justify the use of the words 'same person'.

If we demythologise, however, all these difficulties disappear. It is not for me in this study to argue the advantages and disadvantages of *particular* mythologies; this would require the examination of religious beliefs and practices (e.g. worship of the Virgin Mary) in their full historical context. The important point for our purposes seems to me to be this: what is being talked about is not the literal appearance of a hitherto 'non-material' Virgin Mary but a myth or parable in which the actual Virgin Mary plays a part. Similarly, if people claim to have experienced 'the presence of the risen Christ', this is not a literal reference to a 'non-material' Christ who has existed since A.D. 29 in a 'non-material world' from which he occasionally emerges (as might the man in the top flat in our fable – see Chapter 4); it is a myth or parable involving reference to the actual Jesus Christ who genuinely died somewhere around the year A.D. 29. In this case the demand that people should allow the spirit of Christ to work in their hearts carries many practical consequences; and it can fairly be argued that recognition of the compelling nature of this demand is more important than acceptance of the mythology in which it is expressed. In my own view the mythology can be dispensed with as long as the cosmic significance of the demand is fully recognised.

My conclusion in this chapter is that it is possible to take people's accounts of their religious experiences seriously without having to accept the dualistic contrast between 'material reality' and 'non-material reality' and without having to suppose that, for instance, Jehovah, Jesus Christ or the Virgin Mary sometimes appear to people in 'non-material' form.

6 The 'Natural'–'Supernatural' Dichotomy

The discussion so far has been concerned in particular with the issues of 'dualism' and 'materialism'. My argument has been that in many contexts the alleged contrast between 'material' and 'non-material' makes no sense and that the notion of 'two kinds of reality' (or indeed of any other number of 'kinds of reality') is often misleading. In this chapter, I shall try to show the absurdity of asking whether religious experiences have a 'natural' or a 'supernatural' origin, and I shall suggest that the 'natural'–'supernatural' dichotomy is open to precisely the same objections as the 'material'–'non-material' dichotomy.

It is, I think, popularly supposed that if religious experiences can be shown to have a 'natural' origin they can be dismissed as aberrations, whereas if they are of 'supernatural' origin they require to be taken seriously. On this view one would, for instance, take seriously the experience of St Paul on the Damascus road if one believed it to be 'supernaturally caused', whereas if the causes were 'natural' one would dismiss it as some kind of delusion. Christianity, on this view, is tied to 'belief in the supernatural'; if a phenomenon can be explained in 'natural' terms, one is in effect 'explaining it away' and hence discrediting any claims to religious significance which it might otherwise seem to possess.

It is perhaps worth while at this point to quote a particular example of a religious discussion where this popular assumption has apparently been accepted quite uncritically by one of the participants. In a recent article in the *Observer*, John Heilpern wrote of a conversation which he had with Michael Ramsey, Archbishop of Canterbury. After hearing the Archbishop speak of goodness, love, self-sacrifice, humility and beauty as 'absolutes', Heilpern asked, 'Wasn't it conceivable that a saintly man, *and not a supernatural force*, could think up these values?'[1] (my italics). The wording of the question suggests that, for Heilpern, the activity of a saintly man and the activity of a supernatural force are alternative hypotheses (in a quite literal sense) and that he supposes that a Christian archbishop is necessarily committed to belief in the latter.[2]

Now if the problem of validating religious experience is posed in these terms, a would-be defender of religion may well feel threatened in case *all* apparently religious experiences are explained away as delusions. Thus if it is assumed that the only religious experiences which should be taken seriously are 'supernaturally caused' ones, and if it is also assumed that on scientific grounds one must continue to look for 'natural' causes, the conclusion is inevitable that no religious experience should ever be taken seriously. On this showing 'religion' and 'science' are in head-on conflict, since the former requires us to look for 'supernatural' causes while the latter forbids it.

This whole argument seems to me extremely muddled. I do not doubt that, if Christianity were tied to a crude supernaturalism, like that of Invictus in my fable (see above, pp. 27 *seq*.), it would be difficult to be both a bona fide scientist and a Christian. As I see the situation, however, the important thing for a scientist is not to *accept* the 'natural'–'supernatural' dichotomy and then limit himself to studying 'natural' events, but not to use this pair of terms at all. The general principle is this: if one member of a pair of opposed terms marks no worthwhile distinction, then the other member is otiose also.

That the 'natural'–'supernatural' dichotomy serves no purpose in the search for causal explanations can be shown as follows. In all situations where there are two conflicting hypotheses, one hypothesis must necessarily carry different predictions from the other (since this is what is meant by saying that they are in conflict). If in a particular case we are unsure whether or not a particular religious experience was 'supernaturally caused', it follows that there must be some differential prediction which distinguishes the 'supernatural-cause' hypothesis from the 'natural-cause' one. But what are the characteristics of a 'supernatural cause'? Any positive characteristics which are specified will clearly be 'natural' ones; and it seems that the best one can do here is to call the occurrence 'supernatural' in the *absence* of any causal explanation. In that case, however, the expression 'supernatural cause' is simply a name for our ignorance; as an explanation it is vacuous – as vacuous as the *vertus dormitiva* ('sleep-giving virtue') postulated by Molière's medical student to explain why opium sends people to sleep. Vacuous explanations are not merely useless; they are actively misleading, since they imply that an explanation has been given when this is not the case.[3]

Moreover, if one is entitled to take St Paul seriously only if his conversion experience was 'supernaturally caused', those who wish on religious grounds to take him seriously must necessarily have a stake in people's *failure* to find a natural cause; and it is surely an obscurantist form of religion which depends for its truth on gaps in our historical or medical knowledge.[4] This particular difficulty is made less obvious than it might be by the fact that the existing historical evidence is sparse and the prospects of discovering any major new evidence about St Paul are fairly remote. As a result, the 'supernaturalist' will tend to emphasise that a convincing 'natural' explanation of St Paul's behaviour is unlikely to be found, while the 'naturalist', unable to refute him conclusively, will continue to suggest, without any decisive evidence, perhaps that he was an epileptic or was overwhelmed by guilt feelings because of his persecution of the Christians. Clearly neither side will convince the other; and it seems to me to be a deadlock as fatuous as that between Humanist and Invictus in my fable (see above, p. 28).

To add to the confusion there is the notorious logical difficulty over establishing any kind of negative conclusion. Thus to prove that, say, a certain drug does no harm, one gives it to a sample of people and compares their subsequent ailments with those of a matched control group who did not receive the drug. Even, however, if there turns out to be no obvious difference between the two groups, a critic may still be tempted to say, 'But was your sample large enough? Have you really taken sufficient precautions? Might there not be adverse effects which your survey has failed to show up?' In the case of any particular survey this could well be fair comment. If, however, such objections are raised after every survey, one is finally entitled to ask the objector what standards of certainty he is looking for; the comment, 'Perhaps there is *still* something which you have overlooked', carries less and less weight with each survey which fails to show a difference between the two groups. Indeed if such objections are carried to extremes they become misleading, since the objector is trying to carry conviction by saying 'My opponent has not really proved his case', while deceiving his hearers (and perhaps himself) by setting standards of proof that are unattainable. Since in practice there is usually no undisputed criterion of certainty, it is possible for two people to range themselves on opposite sides of a dispute when they both have access to precisely the same evidence. In this particular case those who profess a predilection for 'natural' explanations are likely to insist that there must be *some* 'natural' explanation for St Paul's experience even though they do not know what it is, while those with a stake in excluding 'natural' explanations will be much readier to declare such explanations lacking and will tend to make a more perfunctory search. The situation is not unlike that described by Wittgenstein when he writes: 'If I am inclined to suppose that a mouse has come into being by spontaneous generation out of grey rags and dust, I shall do well to examine those rags very closely to see how a mouse may have hidden in them, how it may have got there, and so on. But if I am convinced that a mouse cannot come into being from these things, then this investigation will perhaps be superfluous.'[5]

One also hears it suggested that 'natural' explanations are to be preferred on grounds of economy. This, however, gives no clear indication of when and why economy is justified. There is an old maxim called 'Occam's razor' – *'entia non sunt multiplicanda praeter necessitatem'* ('entities should not be multiplied beyond what is necessary'); and it seems clear that a simple theory – one which involves a relatively small number of explanatory concepts – is in general preferable to a more complex one. At most, however, Occam's razor tells us only that we should not go beyond what is *necessary*, and it is logically not surprising if supporters of 'supernatural' explanations insist that such explanations *are* necessary. As in my fable (p. 28 above), the argument ends in deadlock.

There is an extra complication here over the term 'entity'. That we should be parsimonious with explanatory principles seems reasonable; to tell people not to multiply *things*, on the other hand, is clearly a preposterous maxim. Indeed it would be grotesque to interpret Occam's razor as though it were advice to rabbit-breeders! Clearly no general maxims of this kind can tell you the extent to which you should encourage your rabbits to 'multiply'. Nor is it being suggested that one should pretend there is only one rabbit in a hutch when in fact there are two. It is perhaps a faulty assimilation to this kind of situation which led Sherrington, the neurologist, to say, 'That our being should consist of *two* fundamental elements offers, I suppose, no greater inherent improbability than that it should rest on one only'.[6] The same mistake, too, seems to have led people to criticise 'the materialist' as a blinkered individual who has failed to look for the 'supernatural' world and limits himself to the 'natural' one; in the background lurks the analogy with the rabbit-keeper who has failed to look properly for a second rabbit in addition to the first one. Both materialists and their opponents seem to me to be guilty of this mistake.

All the above difficulties and disputes are the direct consequence of posing the question in terms of whether religious experiences do or do not have a 'supernatural' cause. The basic mistake is to suppose that the value of St Paul's life and work – or the life and work of any other person whose religious experiences are on record – is in any way tied up with questions of 'supernatural causation'. New facts about a person's life may sometimes lead us to revise our assessment of that person; for instance, if we discovered that a religious teacher regularly suffered from a mental illness such as depression, this might in some cases lead us to look at his life and work in a new way and perhaps value it less. But in the last resort there is no escape from having to assess his religious teaching on its merits. This is a matter of personal responsibility, and there is no easy answer.

One final point requires discussion. It may be objected that the argument in this study proves too much. Is it not the case, it may be said, that in the Christian tradition God has been thought of as a 'supernatural' being or as a 'non-material' causal agency? If, therefore, one rejects the 'natural'–'supernatural' dichotomy, is not this to give up belief in God altogether? The view put forward in this study is in that case a disguised form of atheism.

Now I do not think that believers need be put off by the scare-word 'atheist'. If by the word 'God' is meant 'that supernatural agency which sometimes acts causally in the world', then those who claim to believe in such an entity are deceiving themselves with words; they have failed to see that no evidence could ever provide a use for such an expression. To profess belief in such an entity seems to me neither reverent nor religious; it is as though someone expressed the hope that he would one day discover a married bachelor.

In present-day Christian thinking, however, it is widely agreed that sentences containing the word 'God' cannot and should not be taken literally. John Robinson, for example, has done much to popularise this view; and he seems to me quite correct in not wishing to interpret belief in God as 'being persuaded of the "existence" of some entity, even a supreme entity, which might or might not be there, like life on Mars'.[7] Moreover I can see no consistency in the position of those who say that expressions such as 'Here is the finger of God'[8] or 'sitteth at the right hand of God'[9] are not to be taken literally but that the key words 'existence' and 'cause' when used of God *are* to be taken literally. Indeed since we have presumably learned how to use the words 'finger' and 'right hand' by hearing others use them in the familiar circumstances of ordinary life, it is hard to see how the case could be any different with the words 'existence' and 'cause'. The issue here is not *whether* we learned how to use these words as a result of happenings early in life, but what *particular* happenings give us grounds for using them. The words 'existence' and 'cause' differ from the words 'finger' and 'hand' not because we have learned to use them in the presence of 'non-material' causal agencies, but because the occasions for their use are more subtle and complex.

Because of the absurdity of language which purports literally to describe such agencies, I suggested in an earlier work[10] that the traditional Christian talk of God was to be described as parable-language. On more recent consideration this seems to me to be an unnecessarily provocative thing to say, and to involve a shift in the meaning of the word 'parable' which at the time I did not fully recognise. I still insist, however, that those who interpret 'God'-sentences literally are either adopting some very primitive form of religion, like Euethes in my fable (see above, p. 27), or else deceiving themselves with words. Despite possible reservations over the word 'parable', therefore, my original formula, 'silence qualified by parables', still seems to me helpful. In attempting to come to terms with cosmic questions there is in the last resort no alternative to silence, as indeed has been recognised in many different religious traditions;[11] and where all words are inadequate I take the view that silence can sometimes be more reverent than speech.

There is, of course, nothing new in saying that 'God'-language is not literal; and I differ from some of the more traditional present-day religious thinkers only in insisting that the words 'exist' and 'cause' are as much non-literal as the words 'finger' and 'right hand'.

My conclusion is that rejection of the 'material'–'non-material' dichotomy or the 'natural'–'supernatural' dichotomy presents difficulties only if one takes 'God'-sentences literally – only, that is, if one thinks of God as a 'non-material Being' who exists (or does not exist) in a quite literal sense. I fully agree with John Robinson[12] that Christianity need not be presented in these terms.

7 Experience and Commitment

One of the main characteristics of the view which I have been attacking is the supposition that religious experiences constitute evidence for the activity of a 'non-material' or 'supernatural' reality, namely God. If this were correct, then the justification for religious commitment would rest fairly and squarely on *evidence*. Thus if the evidence showed that it was genuinely this 'non-material' Being who speaks to people in their religious experiences, then for such people commitment is justified and indeed mandatory; if, on the other hand, there is really 'no one there', then the case for commitment breaks down.

There are many situations in ordinary life which are of this kind. Thus, if a person is satisfied by the evidence that heavy cigarette-smoking increases the risk of lung cancer, and if he wishes at all costs to avoid lung cancer, then logically he is committed to the policy of giving up heavy smoking. Similarly, if a person is satisfied by the evidence that a certain drug is harmful, and if he wishes to avoid those harmful effects, he is logically committed to giving up the drug.

There may, of course, be occasions where one is unsure how the evidence should be interpreted. In this connection I cannot resist quoting a story told of Bertrand Russell, according to which he was asked, shortly before his death, what he would say if he suddenly found himself rushed through the gates of heaven into the presence of his Maker. He replied: 'I should say, "Lord, you didn't give us enough evidence!"'' This seems to me a clear-headed appreciation of how evidence should influence our decisions. If the religious issue were as Invictus portrayed it in Chapter 4 above – if, that is, we are called on to decide whether the evidence from religious experience is or is not sufficient to justify belief in a 'non-material' Being – then what Russell says about evidence is completely to the point. Two people, confronted by the same evidence, may sometimes disagree as to what conclusion should be drawn, but (as Russell in effect implies) there is nothing reprehensible in doing one's best with the evidence available; if later evidence shows that one was in fact mistaken in concluding that so-and-so was the case, it does not follow that one was wrong to come to this conclusion in the light of the evidence available.

If this account is applicable in the case of religious experience and religious commitment, the issue becomes a straightforward factual one: is the evidence *good enough*? Can one say that it is *likely* that a 'non-material' Being occasionally reveals himself?

There seems to me, however, to be two major reasons why it is wrong to think of religious commitment in these terms. The first is the one which has been emphasised throughout this study, viz. that no criteria can be formulated for determining what constitutes 'the activity of a non-material Being'; hence it makes no sense to regard commitment as consequential upon the occurrence of such activity. Secondly, religious claims come to us in the form of demands which are unconditional; yet on this showing commitment would be conditional upon certain facts being the case and could not therefore be unconditional in the requisite way. There may admittedly be occasions when for good reasons we decide to ignore evidence; thus in a particular case we might decide to trust a person even though there is a large amount of evidence which suggests that he is untrustworthy.[1] To act in this way, however, is simply to take a calculated risk. It seems to me quite different and quite absurd to say that when the correct interpretation of the evidence is X, a person ever has an obligation to convince himself that it is Y. Yet we should be driven into this absurdity if we insisted both that people had an unconditional obligation to commit themselves and that they should do so only if the evidence justified it.

Does it follow, then, that the appeal to religious experience carries no weight whatever? Is there nothing in even the most moving experience which would justify a religious view of the world?

I do not think this extreme view is justified. Let us take a particular example. In a well-known passage, Browning's Bishop Blougram says:

> ... There's a sunset touch,
> A fancy from a flower-bell, someone's death,
> A chorus-ending from Euripides,
> And that's enough for fifty hopes and fears.[2]

These lines refer to experiences which people throughout the ages have found to be of cosmic significance – the beauty of the sky and of flowers, the problems raised by death, and the sense of wonder at the glories of artistic creation. I see no justification for saying that people's attitudes to cosmic questions should not be influenced by experiences of this kind.

The precise logical relationship involved, however, is one which I find difficult to characterise. One might perhaps start by saying that such experiences are 'self-authenticating'. By this I mean that they should not be regarded as evidence for something else – that 'God exists', for instance, or that 'man's nature is spiritual'; the situation, as we have seen, is quite unlike that in which noises from the top floor of a flat are evidence that someone lives there. Perhaps a better analogy is that of a musical phrase, heard in a context where its beauty really strikes home. I quote two examples. The first is from Mozart's *Marriage of Figaro*:[3]

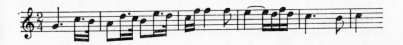

The second comprises the opening bars of the last movement of Beethoven's Fifth Symphony, which comes after a remarkable crescendo at the end of the previous movement:

The music here speaks for itself: it is not 'evidence' for something else.

The same applies in the case of an experience of pictorial art. To quote H. D. Lewis, 'The light in a picture must be the "light that never was on land or sea", for it must make us see what we could not normally see, not necessarily, or indeed usually, by

55

superimposing something on the ordinary sense, but by making us aware of the familiar as we are not normally aware'.[4]

In what sense, then, if at all, can religious experience be compelling? Perhaps one should speak here of *personal* compulsion rather than of *logical* compulsion. If a particular experience strikes home, one's whole way of living may be affected. This is not a rational process, but again it is not an *irrational* process in the sense in which this implies something discreditable.[5] Certain experiences can *invite* a particular answer to cosmic questions; they cannot logically demonstrate that such an answer is correct. To expect more than this is to ask for logical certainty in an area where this cannot be had.

It may, however, be suggested that there is a *de facto* or empirical connection between religious experience and religious commitment. On this view an act of religious commitment could be justified by the fact that certain experiences followed it; for instance, if a person used the words 'I believe' or performed a particular action with symbolic significance (e.g. bowing the head) and then underwent experiences which he called 'feeling the presence of God', this would be evidence, factual evidence, that his commitment was justified.

Such a view seems attractive at first glance, and perhaps seems all the more plausible since it appears to figure in religious literature in a wide variety of contexts. 'O taste and see how gracious the Lord is,' says the psalmist;[6] and the Tate and Brady version contains the lines:

> O make but trial of his love,
> Experience will decide
> How blest are they, and only they,
> Who in his truth confide.

In the well-known verses from *Jesu dulcis memoria* there are the words:

> O hope of every contrite heart
> O joy of all the meek,
> To those who fall, how kind thou art,
> How good to those who seek!

> But what to those who find? Ah! this
> Nor tongue nor pen can show;
> The love of Jesus, what it is
> None but his loved ones know.

56

Similarly in 'Fight the Good Fight' by J. S. B. Monsell there are
the words:

> Only believe and thou shalt see
> That Christ is all in all to thee.

I have certainly come across attempts to present Christianity
in this 'if . . . then' form – if you commit yourself *then* certain
experiences will follow'. I shall try to show, however, that such
attempts involve distortion of the passages which I have quoted.
That religious commitment can correctly be called an 'experiment' I do not dispute; but it is an experiment with a difference.
My main argument will be that if commitment is to count as
religious it needs to be unconditional, in which case no appeal
to consequences is relevant.

I am not, of course, trying here to offer a logical justification
for the policy of religious commitment. What I am offering is
rather an elucidation, in 'persuasive' terms (cf. above, pp. 16–17),
of what is, or should be, involved in the term 'religious'. My
argument does not establish that anyone *ought* to be religious in
this sense; I am saying only that unless the commitment is
unconditional it does not count as religious commitment.

If it is claimed that those who commit themselves do in fact
have certain experiences, the whole problem would become
basically one of fact-finding, and the appropriate terminology
would be that of statistical investigation. I am not saying that
this is an insuperable objection, but such terminology sounds
curious in this context, to say the least. Thus one would presumably lay down criteria of what was to count as 'committing
oneself', with safeguards built in to ensure that the commitment
was genuine; and details would need to be formulated as to the
kinds of experience (joy, peace, etc.) whose occurrence would
lead one to say the result was 'positive'. One would then study
cases of 'commitment' and compare how often they were or
were not followed by the appropriate experiences. Now clearly
this sounds grotesque; and I do not think this is simply because
of practical difficulties in such a research project. I agree it is
sometimes difficult to observe happenings without thereby
altering them; I agree, too, that finding cases of genuine commitment and asking people about them raises all kinds of problems.
The basic cause of discomfort, however, does not seem to me to
lie in these practical difficulties at all; the point is rather that

any such survey, however efficiently carried out, would still be logically irrelevant to the question of justifying religious belief. The terminology of statistical investigation simply does not fit.

The passages quoted, I suggest, should be treated not as scientific generalisations but rather as proclamations. That those who have committed themselves should proclaim what they have experienced after commitment makes good sense. It does the writers less than justice to interpret them as saying, 'Commit yourself *in order to* obtain these experiences'.

The basic point here seems to me a logical one. It is not for me in this study to pre-empt any possible findings of a statistical survey or to express guesses as to what results might occur. My contribution is simply to invite further reflection on what is implied by the term 'religious'. If acts of commitment are carried out with some ulterior objective in mind, then, however commendable such an objective may be, the commitment is not religious.

Let us compare some statements of a more trivial kind which appear to be logically similar. Here are two examples: (i) 'Take the plunge into the swimming-pool; you will enjoy it when you get there'; and (ii) 'Take this medicine; it will do you good'. In both cases the words are of the logical form, 'Do X and Y will follow'.

Now of course commitment to a particular world-view makes a difference in the trivial sense that it would not be genuine commitment if it did not. If someone said, 'I am now committed to Christianity and I do not experience the world any differently', we should be puzzled and might perhaps reply: 'This sounds a very odd form of commitment.' It does not follow, however, that an act of commitment is a device for obtaining new experiences in the way in which, for instance, taking mescalin has been regarded by some people as a device for obtaining new experiences. It is not that commitment always results in new experiences and mescalin sometimes does. The point is rather that the assertion, 'People experience the world differently after commitment', does not represent a scientific generalisation at all; it is simply an attempt to elucidate what the notion of 'commitment' involves.

The difference between the religious statements which I have quoted ('Only believe . . .', etc.) and the 'swimming-pool' and 'medicine' statements is that in the former case the demand is unconditional, whereas in the latter case it is not. It may be, for all I know, that people become less turbulent after becoming religiously committed; but Christianity is not an antidote against turbulence, and the demand 'Follow me'[7] is addressed to the serene and the turbulent alike. Indeed, if this were not so, religious claims would be somewhat like advertisements – 'Commit yourself and you will feel good' – and, like advertisements, they would need to be judged by the relative ratio of successes to failures. Despite certain brands of evangelism, I do not believe that this is the correct way to regard them. On the contrary I agree with Hare[8] that it is not irrational to remain committed even in spite of adverse evidence.

To suppose that religious commitment could ever be justified by an appeal to results is to mistake the nature of what is being demanded. In science, if a research policy does not seem to be leading anywhere, one abandons it; continuation is conditional upon progress. By contrast, the demand in religion for commitment is unconditional; those who commit themselves have no right to expect any particular experiences as a result.

Notes and References

Chapter 1

1. *The Times*, 7 Mar 1970.
2. Ibid., 28 Mar 1970.
3. I. Kant, *Critique of Pure Reason*, trans. N. Kemp Smith (Macmillan, London, 1929) A 750, B 778, p. 600.
4. V. Gollancz, *From Darkness to Light: A Confession of Faith in the Form of an Anthology* (Gollancz, London, 1956).
5. M. Laski, *Ecstasy* (Crescent Press, London, 1961).
6. For further discussion of this point, see below, pp. 21–22.
7. W. James, *The Varieties of Religious Experience* (Longmans, Green, London 1902).
8. Laski, *Ecstasy*.
9. J. L. Austin, *Sense and Sensibilia* (Clarendon Press, Oxford, 1962) p. 3.
10. G. Ryle, *The Concept of Mind* (Hutchinson, London, 1949).
11. Ibid., p. 81.
12. Ibid., p. 69.
13. L. Wittgenstein, *Philosophical Investigations*, trans. G. E. M. Anscombe (Blackwell, Oxford, 1953) § 303.
14. Ibid., § 116. Wittgenstein's use of the word 'metaphysical' in this context is perhaps somewhat mischievous.

Chapter 2

1. Ryle, *The Concept of Mind*, p. 64.
2. E. G. Boring, H. S. Langfeld and W. P. Weld, *Psychology* (Wiley, New York, 1936) pp. 4–7.
3. For further discussion see T. R. Miles, 'The Mental–Physical Dichotomy', *Proceedings of the Aristotelian Society*, LXIV (1964) 71–84.

4. Ryle, *The Concept of Mind*, pp. 22–3.

5. Cf. Austin, *Sense and Sensibilia*, pp. 15–16.

6. For further discussion see B. A. Farrell, 'Experience', *Mind*, n.s., LIX (1950) 170–98, reprinted in V. C. Chappell (ed.), *The Philosophy of Mind* (Prentice-Hall, Englewood Cliffs, N.J., 1962) pp. 23–48.

Chapter 3

1. Lucretius, *De Rerum Natura*, bk I, ll. 62–101.

2. Quoted from A. K. Rogers, *A Student's History of Philosophy* (Macmillan, London, 1912) pp. 397–8. It is interesting that the 1844 translation of Holbach (*The System of Nature*, Cousins, London, 1844) substitutes 'superstition' for 'religion', as does M. F. Smith in his translation of Lucretius (Sphere Books, London, 1969).

3. James i. 27. All biblical quotations are taken from the New English Bible unless an indication is given to the contrary.

4. C. L. Stevenson, *Ethics and Language* (Oxford U.P., 1944). There is, I think, an important difference between expressing certain values and trying to persuade people to adopt these values; and since some of the examples which Stevenson gives seem to involve the former, it is arguable that the word 'persuasive' is a misnomer. As it has gained wide currency in philosophy, however, I have decided to use it rather than coin a fresh term of my own.

5. Ibid., p. 211.

6. Henry Fielding, *Tom Jones*, bk III, chap. 3.

7. C. E. Osgood, G. J. Suci and P. H. Tannenbaum, *The Measurement of Meaning* (Univ. of Illinois Press, Urbana, 1957).

8. I owe the term 'cosmic' to Bishop Ian Ramsey. See, for instance, the passage in chap. 1 of his *Religious Language* (S.C.M. Press, London, 1957) p. 37, where he writes: 'In particular the Christian religion focuses . . . a cosmic commitment on Christ.' Compare also his use of the expression 'cosmic disclosures' (see, for instance, his *Christian Discourse*, Oxford U.P., 1965, p. 5).

9. Psalms viii. 4 (Prayer Book version).

10. E. S. Waterhouse, *The Philosophy of Religious Experience* (Epworth Press, London, 1923), p. 96.

11. F. E. England, *The Validity of Religious Experience* (Ivor Nicholson & Watson, London, 1937) p. 11.

12. In this connection I should like to call attention to the title of Ninian Smart's recent book, *The Religious Experience of Mankind* (Fontana Press, London, 1971). Here Professor Smart presents us with fascinating accounts of many different kinds of religious experience. I was surprised, however, to find that in his opening chapter, 'Religion and Human Experience', he lapses into the kinds of philosophical mistakes which I have been criticising. Thus on p. 12, speaking of St Paul's conversion, he writes: '*This* experience was not observable by others' (my italics). Is he implying that other experiences *might* be observable, and, more important, has he seriously asked himself what are possible uses for the expression 'I am observing an experience'? Moreover, on p. 28 he writes: 'A religious experience involves some kind of "perception" of the *invisible* world, or involves a perception that some visible person or thing is a manifestation of the invisible world' (his italics). If I am right, however, one can take people's religious experiences seriously without talking about an 'invisible world' at all and *a fortiori* without having to explain in what sense such a world is 'perceived'.

13. R. Descartes, *Discourse on Method*, pt. iv.

14. Aristotle, *Categories*.

15. According to Aristotle's classification, 'wisdom' and 'tallness' would count also as being of different ontological status from each other. What words should be grouped together as 'belonging in the same category' depends on the purpose of the classification (cf. J. J. C. Smart, 'A Note on Categories', *Brit. J. Philos. Sci.*, xv 4 (1953) 227–8); but it would be a strange classificatory principle which placed 'house' and 'tallness' in the same category while assigning 'house' and 'stone' to different ones.

16. The examples of 'Wednesday', 'justice' and 'off-side' have been used by Professor Ryle in discussion, and I owe the examples of 'reach' and 'crawl' to Professor Skinner. See B. F. Skinner, *Verbal Behaviour* (Appleton-Century-Crofts, New York, 1957) p. 7.

17. Anselm, *Proslogion*, ii. See J. P. Migne, *Patrologiae Cursus Completus* (1853) clviii, col. 223.

18. T. R. Miles, *Religion and the Scientific Outlook* (Allen & Unwin, London, 1959) pp. 36–46.

19. G. J. Warnock, 'Metaphysics in Logic', *Proceedings of the Aristotelian Society*, li (1950–1) 201.

20. I owe this example to Professor P. T. Geach.

21. Kant, *Critique of Pure Reason*, B 83, p. 97.

Chapter 4

1. Anselm, *Proslogion*, II.

Chapter 5

1. James, *The Varieties of Religious Experience*, pp. 27–8.

2. Quoted from G. M. Hopkins, 'God's Grandeur'.

3. I am grateful to Professor D. Z. Phillips for showing me the significance of this point. See especially D. Z. Phillips, *The Concept of Prayer* (Routledge & Kegan Paul, London, 1965) *passim*.

4. Isaiah vi. 1–8.

5. R. Bultmann, 'New Testament and Mythology'. See chap. 1 of *Kerugma and Myth*, ed. H. W. Bartsch (S.P.C.K., London, 1953).

6. J. A. T. Robinson, *Honest to God* (S.C.M. Press, London, 1963) p. 24.

7. J. A. T. Robinson, *But That I Can't Believe* (Fontana Books, London, 1967) p. 28.

8. Ibid., p. 73.

9. Micah vi. 6–8.

10. John iv. 42.

11. Quoted in *Christian Faith and Practice in the Society of Friends*, §. 20.

12. From Joseph Maréchal, S.J., *Studies in the Psychology of the Mystics*, trans. Algar Thorold (Burns, Oates & Washbourne, London, 1927) pp. 33–4. I am grateful to Professor E. L. Mascall for calling my attention to this work.

13. John iv. 24.

14. 1 John i. 5.

15. 1 John iv. 9.

16. C. B. Martin, *Religious Belief* (Cornell U.P., Ithaca, N.Y., 1959) p. 67.

17. Psalms xxiii. 6 (Prayer Book version).

18. Genesis xxviii. 16.

19. For further discussion see in particular A. G. N. Flew, 'Locke and the Problem of Personal Identity', *Philosophy*, XXVI (1951) 53–68; B. A. O. Williams, 'Personal Identity and Individuation', *Proceedings of the Aristotelian Society*, LVII (1956–7) 229–52; and Martin, *Religious Belief*, chap. 6.

Chapter 6

1. *Observer*, 18 Apr 1971.

2. It is worth noting that in his reply to Heilpern the Archbishop is able to avoid committing himself to any such crude formulation.

3. On p. 2 of *Ecstasy*, Marghanita Laski writes: 'That some such experiences . . . were supernaturally caused it was not my temperamental bias to believe.' If my argument is right, however, the objections to the 'natural'–'supernatural' dichotomy are logically compelling, and personal temperament is therefore irrelevant.

4. For an attack on the notion of a 'God of the gaps', see C. A. Coulson, *Science and Christian Belief* (Fontana Books, London, 1958) pp. 32–3. Cf. also D. M. MacKay, 'Mentality in Machines', *Proceedings of the Aristotelian Society*, suppl. vol. XXVI (1952) p. 86.

5. Wittgenstein, *Philosophical Investigations*, § 52.

6. Quoted by E. D. Adrian in *The Physical Basis of Mind*, ed. Peter Laslett (Blackwell, Oxford, 1950) p. 69.

7. Robinson, *Honest to God*, p. 17.

8. From Robert Browning, *Abt Vogler*.

9. From the Apostles' Creed.

10. Miles, *Religion and the Scientific Outlook*.

11. See, for instance, H. D. Lewis's account of an Indian text which tells of a pupil 'who pleads with his teacher to expound to him the nature of the Absolute Self understood religiously as Brahman. To each request the teacher turns a deaf ear until at last he answers the insistent "Teach me, Sir", with the words "I am teaching you but you do not follow, the Self is silence".' From H. D. Lewis, 'The Cognitive Factor in Religious Experience', *Proceedings of the Aristotelian Society*, supp. vol. XXIX (1955) p. 73. I should like to express my gratitude to Professor

Lewis for what I have learned from him over a period of many years.

12. Robinson, *Honest to God, passim.*

Chapter 7

1. In a characteristically entertaining paper, H. H. Price cites the example of nineteenth-century ladies who thought it their duty to believe that their husbands or fiancés were impeccably virtuous. See H. H. Price, 'Belief and Will', *Proceedings of the Aristotelian Society*, suppl. vol. xxviii (1954) p. 13.

2. Robert Browning, *Bishop Blougram's Apology.*

3. The passage is taken from the aria 'I remember'. See p. 247 of *The Marriage of Figaro*, ed. Boosey and Hawkes (1947).

4. H. D. Lewis, 'On Poetic Truth', *Philosophy*, xxi 79 (1946) 155. This article has been reprinted as chap. 10 of Professor Lewis's book, *Morals and Revelation* (Allen & Unwin, London, 1951); the passage quoted appears on p. 242.

5. Cf. L. Wittgenstein, *Lectures and Conversations on Aesthetics, Psychology, and Religious Belief*, ed. Cyril Barrett (Blackwell, Oxford, 1966) p. 58.

6. Psalms xxxiv. 8 (Prayer Book version).

7. Matthew ix. 9.

8. R. M. Hare, 'Theology and Falsification', published in *New Essays in Philosophical Theology*, ed. A. G. N. Flew and A. C. MacIntyre (S.C.M. Press, London, 1955) pp. 99–103.